THE HAMLYN LECTURES

TWENTIETH SERIES

JUSTICE IN THE WELFARE STATE

AUSTRALIA
The Law Book Company Ltd.
Sydney : Melbourne : Brisbane

CANADA AND U.S.A.
The Carswell Company Ltd.
Agincourt, Ontario

INDIA
N. M. Tripathi Private Ltd.
Bombay

MALAYSIA : SINGAPORE : BRUNEI
Malayan Law Journal (Pte.) Ltd.
Singapore

ISRAEL
Steimatzky's Agency Ltd.
Jerusalem : Tel Aviv : Haifa

NEW ZEALAND
Sweet & Maxwell (N.Z.) Ltd.
Wellington

PAKISTAN
Pakistan Law House
Karachi

JUSTICE IN THE WELFARE STATE

BY

HARRY STREET
Solicitor of the Supreme Court
Professor of English Law in the University of Manchester

SECOND EDITION

Published under the auspices of
THE HAMLYN TRUST

LONDON
STEVENS & SONS
1975

Published in 1975 by
Stevens & Sons Limited
of 11 New Fetter Lane in
the City of London and
printed in Great Britain by
The Eastern Press Limited
of London and Reading

SBN Hardback 420 44450 5
SBN Paperback 420 44460 2

CONTENTS

The Hamlyn Trust ix

1. SOCIAL SECURITY TRIBUNALS 1
   Reasons for the Rise of Administrative Tribunals 2
   Social Security Tribunals in Action . . . 10

2. RENT AND NATIONAL HEALTH SERVICE TRIBUNALS 33
   Rent Control 33
   Rent Act 1974 54
   The Future of Social Security and Rent Tribunals 56
   National Health Service Tribunals 57

3. THE SUPERVISION OF TRIBUNALS 61
   Franks Committee Report 61
   Council on Tribunals 62
   The Inadequacies of Judicial Review . . . 65

4. LICENSING 70
   Reasons for the Growth of Licensing . . . 70
   Disadvantages of Licensing 74
   Who Grants Licences? 79
   Sources of Licensing Power 82
   Registration 83
   Procedures 84
   Judicial Review 88
   Systems of Inspection 89
   Some Needed Reforms 90

5. THE CITIZEN AND WHITEHALL 96
Public Inquiries 96
Decisions by Civil Servants without a Hearing 107
The Parliamentary Commissioner . . . 115
The Administrative Process 124

THE HAMLYN LECTURES

1949 Freedom under the Law
by The Rt. Hon. Lord Denning

1950 The Inheritance of the Common Law
by Richard O'Sullivan, Esq.

1951 The Rational Strength of English Law
by Professor F. H. Lawson

1952 English Law and the Moral Law
by Dr. A. L. Goodhart

1953 The Queen's Peace
by Sir Carleton Kemp Allen

1954 Executive Discretion and Judicial Control
by Professor C. J. Hamson

1955 The Proof of Guilt
by Dr. Glanville Williams

1956 Trial by Jury
by The Rt. Hon. Lord Devlin

1957 Protection from Power under English Law
by The Rt. Hon. Lord MacDermott

1958 The Sanctity of Contracts in English Law
by Sir David Hughes Parry

1959 Judge and Jurist in the Reign of Victoria
by C. H. S. Fifoot, Esq.

1960 The Common Law in India
by M. C. Setalvad, Esq.

1961 British Justice: The Scottish Contribution
by Professor T. B. Smith

1962 Lawyer and Litigant in England
by Dr. R. E. Megarry

1963 Crime and the Criminal Law
by The Baroness Wootton of Abinger

1964 Law and Lawyers in the United States
by Dean Erwin N. Griswold

1965 New Law for a New World?
by The Rt. Hon. Lord Tangley

1966 Other People's Law
by The Hon. Lord Kilbrandon

1967 The Contribution of English Law to South African Law; and the Rule of Law in South Africa
by The Hon. O. D. Schreiner

1968 Justice in the Welfare State
by Professor H. Street

1969 The British Tradition in Canadian Law
by The Hon. Bora Laskin

1970 The English Judge
by Henry Cecil

1971 Punishment, Prison and the Public
by Professor Sir Rupert Cross

1972 Labour and the Law
by Dr. Otto Kahn-Freund

1973 Maladministration and its Remedies
by K. C. Wheare

1974 English Law—The New Dimension
by Leslie Scarman

1975 Justice in the Welfare State (*Second Edition*)
by Professor H. Street

THE HAMLYN TRUST

THE Hamlyn Trust came into existence under the will of the late Miss Emma Warburton Hamlyn, of Torquay, who died in 1941, at the age of eighty. She came of an old and well-known Devon family. Her father, William Bussell Hamlyn, practised in Torquay as a solicitor for many years. She was a woman of strong character, intelligent and cultured, well versed in literature, music and art, and a lover of her country. She inherited a taste for law, and studied the subject. She also travelled frequently on the Continent and about the Mediterranean, and gathered impressions of comparative jurisprudence and ethnology.

Miss Hamlyn bequeathed the residue of her estate in terms which were thought vague. The matter was taken to the Chancery Division of the High Court, which on November 29, 1948, approved a Scheme for the administration of the Trust. Paragraph 3 of the Scheme is as follows:

> "The object of the charity is the furtherance by lectures or otherwise among the Common People of the United Kingdom of Great Britain and Northern Ireland of the knowledge of the Comparative Jurisprudence and the Ethnology of the chief European countries including the United Kingdom, and the circumstances of the growth of such jurisprudence to the intent that the Common People of the United Kingdom may realise the privileges which in law and custom they enjoy in comparison with other European Peoples and realising and appreciating such privileges may recognise the responsibilities and obligations attaching to them."

From the first the Trustees decided to organise courses of lectures of outstanding interest and quality by persons of eminence, under the auspices of co-operating Universities or other bodies, with a view to the lectures being made available in book form to a wide public.

The Twentieth Series of Hamlyn Lectures was originally delivered in November 1968 by Professor H. Street at Liverpool University.

J. N. D. ANDERSON,
Chairman of the Trustees.

March, 1975.

PREFACE

I HAVE left the arrangement of the Hamlyn Lectures in the form in which I originallly delivered them. I have not changed my views substantially since the first edition, but I have tried to take account of the considerable changes in the law, especially legislation, which have taken place in the ensuing six years.

PROFESSOR H. STREET

University of Manchester,
March 1975

CHAPTER 1

SOCIAL SECURITY TRIBUNALS

THE State regulates our lives more than ever before. We look to the State to provide us with security and assistance in so many forms. This is what I mean by the Welfare State. Its effect on all our institutions, and not least on the law, has been tremendous. Its development has greatly increased the potential area of dispute between government and citizen. I regard it as highly important that each and every one of us is dealt with justly in our relations with the State. That is what I am concerned with in these lectures. How have our institutions adjusted themselves to the Welfare State? How successful have we been? What more needs to be done?

I take a look first of all at how we now try to resolve conflicts between officials and the public. If there is a dispute between two people and there has to be a trial to settle it we tend to assume that the ordinary courts will always be the appropriate body to hear the case. And so most of the Hamlyn lectures have been about the law dispensed by the ordinary courts—and that is perfectly understandable. I shall not be talking about that. The law fashioned by other tribunals is now also very important in the British way of life. We are rightly proud of our attempts to create a system of social justice in this country and most of us citizens feel that we know something about it. Perhaps fewer people think about the unique contribution of English law in this sphere—I shall try to fill that gap. To do this I shall have to look at many institutions other than the ordinary courts.

In these days an enormous number of cases is heard and decided by agencies other than the ordinary courts. This is essentially a twentieth-century development. Why has it happened?

Reasons for the Rise of Administrative Tribunals

The Welfare State

We have the main clue once we see that this trend started when Lloyd George pioneered his National Health Insurance Act in 1911. It is the extension of the Welfare State which leads to matters being taken away from the courts. When the State provides benefits for citizens it has to devise machinery for ascertaining who has a good claim. When the State imposes controls there has to be a procedure which ensures that the citizen's freedom is not interfered with in an arbitrary manner. The 1911 Act set up special tribunals to handle contested claims for unemployment benefit. These tribunals worked exceptionally well, so much so that the sceptical became convinced that the judges were not the only ones who could do justice in disputes between the government and the public. These unemployment tribunals became the pattern for many others.

We usually call all these bodies administrative tribunals. The name is a good one. It distinguishes them from the ordinary courts. It also reminds us that it is a question of policy to be resolved by the Administration what arrangements are appropriate for deciding a particular set of claims. For instance, the Government decides to introduce a State scheme of unemployment benefits. It works out how the money is to be raised and prescribes the qualification for benefit, and the manner of making payments. It has to meet the situation where a citizen claims benefit and a government official does not accept this claim. It is purely an administrative matter how the Act is going to handle those contested issues. That matter will be resolved, not by laying it down that because there is a dispute it is a judicial question for a judge, but by asking what in the circumstances is the most efficient manner of performing this administrative task.

Links with government

We can readily see how decisions like that are closely linked with the Administration. Plainly the Administration is going to be responsible for the routine day to day payment of benefits. It will be less than say one case in ten thousand where there is an unresolved doubt about a claim to benefit. The Administration will be inclined to regard that one in ten thousand cases as just another administrative problem—calling for a special solution, yes—but it would be natural for it to think of recourse to some institution connected with the responsible department, rather than for it to say: "This is a judicial issue, which must obviously be decided by one of Her Majesty's judges." What I have just said about benefits is also true of granting a licence to do something or other, or of other ways in which the State now regulates our activities.

What is needed above all else is a cheap and speedy settlement of disputes. For these cases we do not want a Rolls-Royce system of justice. Some would say that there is too much of the Rolls and not enough of the Mini even in much of our trials in the law courts. If the average claim to benefit is less than £10 we do not want a judge on a pensionable salary of over £12,000 a year with all the trappings (so often foisted on unwilling judges) of special judges' lodgings, private butler, police escort, ushers and marshal, to decide the claim. Nor do we want to wait for years to elapse between the making of the claim and the arrival at a final decision.

We can compile a very long list of matters of this kind which have arisen under the Welfare State for decision by administrative tribunals. Claims for unemployment benefit, family allowances, maternity benefits, death grants, industrial injury benefits, sickness benefits, supplementary benefits (the old National Assistance) and all other social security benefits are settled in this way. The Government decides to regulate rents of houses—and so we have rent assessment committees and rent tribunals. We have a nationalised health service; therefore we need tribunals to investigate complaints against doctors, dentists, opticians and chemists within the service. We interfere with the freedom of businesses to carry goods and passengers on the road where they will; tribunals supervise this regulation of road transport. The right of the Englishman to do as he likes with his land is taken away from him because we recognise the superior claims of public bodies to acquire it on payment of compensation—disputes about compensation go to the Lands Tribunal. We protect the employee by giving him certain rights to compensation if he is made redundant; we interfere with the employer's freedom to dismiss him—industrial tribunals are there to apply these new laws. Injured servicemen may be entitled to a pension—pensions appeal tribunals will decide. When there is compulsory national service, claims for postponement of service and for eventual reinstatement in civilian employment are heard by special tribunals. Regional Health Authorities find it necessary to detain under the Mental Health Act 1959 those who suffer from mental illness or disorder; we have mental health review tribunals to review, on the application of the Secretary of State for Social Services, the patient or his nearest relatives, the case of anyone liable to be detained.

The quest for speed, cheapness and efficiency

There are many other explanations for this movement away from the ordinary courts. Ministers and their top civil servant advisers have in this century frequently come to doubt whether the courts are the appropriate body to decide many of these new cases. They see rightly that many of these disputes are not merely about private rights: the public good on the one hand and the interest of the particular citizen on the other must be weighed in the balance. They look at many decisions in the courts, even at the level of the House of Lords, and find them wanting in that they appear to disregard the social element in a problem. For example, the courts have chosen to hold that there is no law against letting a tumble-down house; even though the landlord knew of the defects, he is held by them not to be liable to anybody injured on the premises because of their defective condition. Again, the courts held that traders who were determined to obtain a monopoly were free to combine together in order to drive a rival trader out of business. Administrators asked themselves whether judges who arrived at such decisions could be relied on to show a proper regard for the public interest, which would often be paramount or decisive in cases referred to them.

There was also a lack of confidence in the way in which courts interpreted Acts of Parliament. This was important because the new kinds of decisions were almost always ones where the meaning of a section of an Act had to be found. Our courts have always laid the greatest stress on giving statutes their literal meaning. Unlike courts in most other countries, they are reluctant to examine the underlying purpose of the legislation, so that they will never be prepared to listen to evidence of what the Government's intentions were in introducing the Bill; they even refuse to familiarise themselves with the background to the legislation by reading *Hansard's* reports of the parliamentary proceedings leading to the enactment. Politicians feared that the courts might frustrate the social purposes of their Acts if they approached cases in this constricted literal fashion. A more serious charge has been levelled at the judges; that they brought to statutory interpretation nineteenth-century notions of the inviolability of property; that they would lean over backwards to find that a statute had not taken away an individual's property rights, even if expropriation for public purposes on payment of compensation was the cardinal aim of the Act. Of course it does not matter whether these suspicions and attitudes of our politicians and civil servants were well-founded; I am looking for the reasons why they diverted topics away from the judges. I am not saying that all their reasons were valid.

Whatever his other faults, the politician or civil servant is sometimes prepared to admit that he might have been wrong, and to change his mind. Flexibility is seen as a key attribute in a decision-maker. Yet the courts have long had a different approach: that once a decision has been reached in a case, it should be a binding precedent for other judges to follow in similar future cases. If the new class of cases had been tried by the courts, principles would have become rigid; courts would have to do for evermore what their predecessors had done, even though they were convinced that the earlier decisions were wrong. It was thought that this judicial inflexibility was inappropriate for many of the new kinds of decision.

The ordinary judge has to be a jack of all trades. This week he may try a murderer, and next week he may hear successively running-down claims, industrial accidents, claims by a deceived house buyer for recovery of his purchase price, and actions for breach of contract to deliver goods. Many of the new State schemes are extraordinarily complex; mastery of the laws can be obtained only by intense specialisation. Governments therefore thought it wise to set up tribunals specially to handle cases under any one particular item of social legislation; they felt that judges who were general practitioners could not be expected to have the necessary expertise and ready familiarity with these detailed new provisions. Sometimes it was considered that the necessary consistency of decision could be attained only if all cases were decided by the same person. Rent tribunals are an obvious example. Nobody would pretend that the reasonable rent of a furnished house or flat can be determined with mathematical precision. Public confidence would be lost if, say, comparable flats in the same block were given markedly different rent ceilings—we know how magistrates are criticised for having different ideas about fines for road traffic offences such as speeding. Continuity and consistency of decision should ensue if the same personnel make decisions in a given area.

There is another less obvious but equally important reason for the development of administrative tribunals. The High Court judge and the lawyer who practises before him have an instinctive yearning for certainty; they like their law to be cut and dried, to have it settled once and for all so that lawyers and their clients know exactly where they stand. There is a lot to be said for this view. We are all entitled to know, for instance (or to have our solicitor tell us), whether what we propose to do is a crime. If we buy a house, we do not want to be told that in the present state of the law it is uncertain whether we shall acquire a good title to it. But the administrators maintain that they cannot run the modern State like that. They talk of the formulation of standards. They see a stage between a fixed rule and anarchy. They find it impossible to legislate in advance for every specific instance. For them decision-making is not then some mechanical process; one cannot use a slot machine or even a computer in order to obtain the answer. In their statutes they use words like " fair," " adequate " and " reasonable," intending that these standards shall be applied to particular cases in the light of experience. They doubt whether judges will find it congenial to work in this way. They also observe that when judges have in the past had to handle such concepts they have been prone to crystallise what should have been merely instances of the standard into rigid legal rules from which they would depart only with reluctance. For instance, courts which had to decide whether a motorist was driving with reasonable care would be tempted to say, once it had been held that a motorist was liable for not being able to pull up within the range of his lights, that a new rule of law had emerged for all circumstances—that it was always careless not to be able to pull up within the limits of one's vision.

Whitehall did not want this to happen to their administrative standards. They see them as flexible. Take some examples from modern administrative schemes. Are premises educationally suitable? Is a building of special architectural interest? Has a man capacity for work? Is employment available in a district? We see that not only must these standards be developed in the light of experience; technical experts must assist in applying them. The working out of these from case to case is not for lawyer-judges alone; the educationist, the architect, the town planner, the valuer, the industrialist and the trade union official have to participate in this task. Neither politicians nor the judges themselves regarded the courts as ideally equipped for duties of this kind.

The judging process in many of these areas demands an adaptability which judges are not accustomed to display. A local valuation court is not content to sit back and listen to what the house owner and rating officer tell them about the rateable value of the house; it members go and see for themselves. A social security tribunal dealing with a claim for industrial injuries can interrupt the hearing for half an hour to go and visit the scene of the accident. Judges do not do this kind of thing (at least publicly); those who decide these new kinds of dispute must.

A related point is the traditional passiveness of courts—they act only when someone takes the initiative in bringing matters before them. If supervision is to be effective, then sometimes representatives of the administrative agency must unearth wrongdoers and bring them before the agency for a hearing. This approach is commonplace in America in such matters, for example, as monopolies, restrictive practices and false advertising, and there are signs that we may follow in some spheres of administrative control.

Unless a litigant engages a lawyer he is never at ease in court. The judge is aloof, the procedure is formal, there is an atmosphere of uncomfortable dignity. A man likes to be able to have his say in his own way, unrestrained by the niceties of the rule against hearsay evidence and the rest. He does not want to be reprimanded every time—and it will be often—that he fails to distinguish between cross-examining a witness and making a point in his own favour. Administrative tribunals are sufficiently informal to permit these liberties; courts never are. Many believe that a man ought not to be compelled to pay for legal representation in order to get a fair hearing of his case.

I am not passing strictures on the courts. I have been trying to explain why so many Bills are enacted which entrust powers to new administrative tribunals. The courts may have been misjudged; they may have been able to carry out some of these tasks satisfactorily. Yet Whitehall thought that other bodies could do better, and I have tried to explain why. Whereas functions are transferred from court to tribunals because of judicial shortcomings (whether real or assumed), once an administrative tribunal is set up, it appears to give such satisfaction that it is never replaced by the ordinary courts. This matter is not a conflict between the administration and the judges. The judges, like everyone else, desire that the country's policies be carried out fairly and efficiently. They are not hostile to administrative tribunals; on the whole they accept them as a necessity. At most they will insist that disputes ordinarily ought to be tried in the courts, and that a powerful case should be made out before they are entrusted to other agencies.

So far I have been talking rather abstractly about administrative justice. Now I am going to look closely at some administrative tribunals. I will concentrate on those of which I have first-hand experience. Most of us are likely at some time or other to be concerned with claims for social security benefit, and I shall examine in detail how those claims are handled.

Social Security Tribunals in Action

I have mentioned already that bodies have been adjudicating on cases of this type since 1911. Before 1946 there was an extraordinary jumble of separate arrangements for dealing with the various benefits: sickness, unemployment, pensions and the like. Those benefits were dispensed by organisations of the State. Workmen's compensation for accidents at work had been handled quite separately since it was introduced in 1897. Workmen's compensation was treated as purely a private matter between employer and workman. If the workman showed that he had suffered "personal injury by accident arising out of and in the course of employment" he had a claim even though the employer was not at fault. All disputed claims were tried by the ordinary courts in the usual way. Even though this system gave injured workmen more rights than they had enjoyed before its administration by the courts proved disastrous. For instance, thousands of cases were taken to appeal on one point alone: the meaning of "personal injury by accident arising out of and in the course of employment." Writers of textbooks on workmen's compensation made a fortune by bringing out a new edition every year to deal with the mass of case law; law publishers produced special series of law reports every month. The insurance companies who were covering employers' liability took innumerable cases to the House of Lords, despite protests by that House. The struggle between wealthy insurance companies and the worker (not all of whom were members of a trade union) was manifestly unequal at a time when there was no legal aid. Lawyers specialised in workmen's compensation cases, and some even became judges who had been spending virtually all their professional lives in workmen's compensation litigation. The law became extremely complicated and detailed, and bitterness between workmen and employers resulted. The failure of this attempt to treat the problem as a private contest between individuals made replacement inevitable once the Beveridge Committee had been set up in the last war to review the social services. As part of its proposals for a major reform of social security arrangements, that Report recommended a universal State scheme of insurance against injury at work. What has emerged is a comprehensive parliamentary scheme of social security administered by the Department of Health and Social Security. There is a uniform machinery for handling claims to the various forms of benefit: sickness benefit, retirement pensions, death grants, family allowances, industrial injury benefits, maternity benefits, unemployment benefits, widow's benefits, guardians' allowances and child's special allowance.

Machinery

Every claim for benefit is decided in the first instance by an insurance officer. Insurance officers are appointed by the Secretary of State for Social Services to act at local offices of that Ministry; insurance officers for claims to unemployment benefit are appointed at local employment exchanges by that Minister with the concurrence of the Secretary of State for Employment and Productivity. Those insurance officers decide about 18 million claims in an average year. An appeal lies from their decision to local tribunals of which there are 193 in this country. They hear some 35,000 appeals in a year. Appeals from local tribunals lie to the Chief Commissioner or one of the Commissioners, who decide over 2,000 appeals a year. Medical questions involving the assessment of disablement for the purposes of the Industrial Injuries Scheme are decided by independent medical boards with an appeal to one of twelve medical appeal tribunals. These tribunals decide about 15,000 cases a year; in certain cases a further appeal on a point of law lies to a Commissioner.

Procedure

So much for the facts and statistics. What happens in practice? The insurance officer decides cases entirely on paper evidence; he does not ordinarily interview claimants and he never sees witnesses. Department inspectors will at his request collect statements for him. Perhaps in one case in thirty thousand, and those almost entirely industrial injuries and unemployment benefit cases, he believes that because of conflicting evidence he cannot decide himself and refers it to the local tribunal for decision. Whenever he rejects a claim he sends the claimant a brief note to that effect and informs him of his right to appeal within 21 days. Any disappointed claimant can appeal, and it costs him nothing; he merely has to fill in a form stating that he is appealing. About two or three months later the local tribunal will hear his appeal, usually in the premises of the local office of the Department. The tribunal has no control over the hearing lists; it has no power to speed up sittings. It merely attends for hearings when summoned by the clerk.

Membership

A local tribunal consists of three members. The chairman is usually a lawyer, and the Lord Chancellor and the Minister must concur in his being appointed. He is authorised to act as chairman anywhere in the country, but is ordinarily assigned to one locality. Before he is appointed he is vetted at an interview with a senior official from the regional office of the Department. He is normally over 35 years old, and is expected to have acquaintance with working class life and conditions. Close political affiliations are undesirable. The impression is given to the interviewee that others are being considered and that the views of local citizens in public life will be sought. The other two members are appointed from two panels. One member will be from a panel which represents employers and the self-employed. The other member is drawn from a panel representing those who are employed. Appropriate local organisations nominate names, and the Minister appoints. The employee's panel consists almost entirely of trade union officials. The employers and self-employed panel has very few employers on it; it is made up mostly of middle-range executives, especially personnel officers, and a few virtually retired employers. The clerk to the tribunal selects one member from each panel for each sitting. If practicable, there is to be a woman member whenever a claimant is a woman: the Act does not insist on this, and the clerk is often unable to provide a woman member. The panels may be large, and years may elapse before the same three members sit together again.

Hearings

Before the hearing the members and the claimant are each sent the same set of papers on the case. These consist of the insurance officer's decision, the claimant's notice of appeal, the insurance officer's version of the facts, any written evidence obtained, and a detailed submission by the insurance officer which supports with appropriate legal authorities his original decision. The chairman is not consulted beforehand about what evidence should be made available at the hearing; when he arrives at the hearing he will learn for the first time whether particular witnesses, for example, an employer in a claim for unemployment benefit, have been invited by the insurance officer to attend. The tribunal has no power to subpoena witnesses and cannot take evidence on oath.

The Department issues to each chairman about 18 bulky volumes which contain the statutes, statutory instruments, a few of the cases decided by the Commissioner, and digests of those cases. He is also issued with Notes for Guidance prepared by the Department. It is his responsibility to annotate and keep up to date his set of these highly complex materials which consist of many thousands of pages of law relating solely to social security benefits. He is handicapped by the tardiness of the Department in keeping him up to date; six months' arrears are commonplace for his copies. Nobody has ever attempted to write comprehensive textbooks on this branch of the law, so that the chairman has to rely on those materials as he prepares for hearings. They can be bought by any member of the public at Her Majesty's Stationery Office. Insurance officers are also provided with a manual, which is never seen by tribunals. This is to guide them in the discharge of their duties and in the preparation of cases for appeal.

A clerk to the tribunal will normally put on seven cases for a half-day hearing. Hearings are advertised; the public and Press are entitled to attend, unless the chairman rules in a particular case that intimate personal or financial circumstances, or considerations of public security, necessitate a hearing in private. The Press never attend, and the public seldom.

At a hearing the claimant, the insurance officer and the Minister are entitled to be heard. Everybody who is entitled to be heard is allowed to be represented by another person, who need not be a lawyer. I have never known the Minister to appear or to be represented. In employment cases the insurance officer is sometimes present, but is often represented by another insurance officer who specialises in preparing cases before local tribunals; in important cases (always in "trade dispute" test cases) an official of the regional office will represent the insurance officer. In more than half of the appeals the insurance officer has in the past neither appeared nor been represented. A claimant is almost never represented unless he is a trade unionist, when he will then frequently have the help of a local officer of his union. In about one case in a thousand a claimant will be represented by a solicitor (counsel are almost never briefed), and he will be represented by an unadmitted clerk from a solicitor's office in about two cases in a thousand.

In almost one half of the cases the claimant fails to appear at the hearing, often without explanation. The tribunal decides whether to adjourn or proceed. Where the insurance officer has disqualified the claimant for unemployment benefit, it not infrequently happens that a director or manager of his former employer's firm attends as a witness at the appeal only to find that the employee does not appear.

The tribunal does everything possible to make claimants feel at ease. The proceedings are conducted around a table in a most informal way. Often the point at issue is an abstruse legal one, and it is impossible to expect the claimant to handle it. The chairman does all he can to help the claimant to put his case; he can hardly avoid being both claimant's friend and also an adjudicator. Often the panel members are remarkably successful in extracting evidence from nervous and diffident claimants who find it difficult to express themselves. Trade union representatives are a great help to the proceedings if—and this does not happen often enough—the claimant member has briefed them upon adequate notice. The insurance officer often exercises his right to question claimant or witnesses. He seldom wishes to add to his written submission. He does not regard himself as bound at all costs to defend his decision. I am always impressed by the fair-mindedness of insurance officers. If the evidence, or indeed legal discussion, on the appeal shows their decision to have been wrong, they will normally volunteer an admission of that. I have never known an officer bully or hector a claimant.

The tribunal (and in practice that means the chairman) records in writing the evidence submitted—this is not required by law, but there is an official form expressly for that purpose and the Notes for Guidance of Chairmen states that he is required to do it. When the evidence and argument are concluded, all persons other than the clerk are required to withdraw, while the tribunal deliberates. Almost always the tribunal, before proceeding to the next case, then reaches its decision, which may be by a majority. Some might have feared that in unemployment and industrial injury benefit cases the trade union member would sometimes lean over backwards to favour claimants, but this does not happen. Equally, the other member shows no tendency to oppose those claimants. Dissenting judgments are rare, and would no doubt be rarer still if there were anything like the old-style jury room pressure to reach unanimity. The tribunal has to record the facts which it has found and its reasons for decision, and copies of these are sent to the parties. Accordingly, it does not deliver an oral judgment, although its clerk informs the claimant of the result at once on a prescribed form; no doubt this practice, a relic from the time when the Press and public were not allowed to be present, partly explains why the Press never attend. A hearing without a judgment is not attractive copy.

Some typical cases

I have said nothing yet about the kinds of cases dealt with. At almost every sitting there will be a case or two where an employee has been disqualified for unemployment benefit, either on the ground that he has been dismissed for misconduct, or because he has voluntarily left his employment without just cause. These cases plunge one into the heart of the day-to-day industrial life of the nation, and it is a great help to have worked on the factory floor. Demarcation disputes, clocking on, rows with the foreman, bad timekeeping, working conditions, absenteeism: these are typical issues. If the labourer is allowed by the foreman to go to the betting shop to lay bets for the men, and he stays at the shop for the result of the race, to be dismissed by the managing director who sees him leaving the shop, is that misconduct? Did the driver refuse to drive the van because the brakes were defective? Was the West Indian driver who was told to deliver a load to Newcastle at fault when he headed for the Potteries? Must a man who has to stay off work through illness make sure that his boss is telephoned the same day? Did an immigrant, who had been a printer in his own country, and who could only obtain union recognition here by getting a footing in the printing trade, act with just cause when he gave up a regular labouring job for a temporary job with a printer? Should a baker of 20 years' standing be treated as dismissed for misconduct when a knife was found in dough? Was the long-distance lorry driver dismissed for not looking after his load or because he refused to be on driving duty for hours longer than those permitted by the Road Traffic Act? If a railway signalman is convicted of committing an indecent act in a public place during his off-duty hours, is that misconduct?

At most sittings the tribunal will try industrial injuries cases, which are commonly regarded as the most important. The question will often be whether the claimant suffered personal injury caused by accident arising out of and in the course of his employment. A cleaner slips on the icy pavement outside the store where she was about to work one morning. A corporation gardener travels by bus from one park to another in the course of his duties; he ends his work at Park 1 at lunch-time, goes a quarter of a mile home to eat; while proceeding by bus to Park 2 he falls off the platform. Is his case different from that of the painter in the following circumstances? He had to spend one particular working day decorating a certain house. It was his practice to cycle to wherever he was working. To reach this house he had to cycle past his employer's premises. Having passed them, he was knocked off his cycle before reaching the house where he was to work. An elderly night-worker in a factory likes to put his feet up in the middle of the night break. He doesn't go out to the canteen, instead he remains in the machine shop, sits on one metal chair, and is about to lift his feet on to a second chair when, owing to the greasy condition of the floor, the first chair slips from under him. It is obviously no easy matter to decide when the accident arises in the course of employment.

Frequently there is the even more difficult task of deciding whether there has been an accident. Granted that the claimant is disabled, is that because he slipped three years ago when carrying something heavy? Has the hospital ward helper back trouble through lifting a patient or because she had some pre-existing disc defect or arthritis? Although these issues obviously have a medical element it is the tribunal alone which must decide them. The Department will have had the claimant examined within the Department by a general practitioner, and that report will be available; the Department never brings the examining doctor as a witness before the tribunal. A claimant seldom brings a medical witness; pathetically, the most he usually does (if he is unassisted) is to bring a copy of his general practitioner's sick note, with its three-word explanation. If he is a trade unionist and the union is reasonably wealthy and believes the case important enough, the union will furnish a consultant's report. Even though the claimant has been seen regularly by a hospital consultant or registrar he seldom thinks of seeking a report from him; the tribunal is free to adjourn and may help him get a report from that source, for which the Department will pay a fee of £7·85. It may be asked how a lay tribunal presumes to decide these medical questions when no doctors even appear before it. The chairman has an uncontrolled discretion to ask for a medical assessor. An assessor will be a general practitioner, never an expert in the relevant disease—his fee is £3·95. In practice the Department finds it difficult to attract even general practitioners to come in specially and often has to rely on doctors who are doing other medical examinations for the Department finishing early and helping in this case. The assessor is merely an adviser, and is not allowed by the regulations to take part in the decision. The Commissioner has further ruled that the assessor can neither ask nor be asked questions about the case. His advice must be tendered in the presence of the parties, who are given the opportunity to comment.

Another frequent issue on industrial injuries is whether a claimant shall be awarded a special hardship benefit of up to £6·56 a week, because in consequence of his accident his ability to earn has been reduced. These questions are often difficult. One needs to know what are the current earnings of someone engaged on the claimant's former job and how much he is now capable of earning. It is particularly difficult to decide what a semi-skilled, partially disabled middle-aged woman is now capable of earning. Again medical questions are frequently raised. A Department medical board may state that the claimant is either fit for his previous job or soon will be, whereas the claimant says that he can no longer grip and carry his moulding trays, or that his back prevents him from standing up to a day's labouring. Somehow or other, one has to balance the medical opinions, the claimant's testimony and one's knowledge of his occupation. He is a bold man who knows that he has always arrived at the right result in cases of this type.

Many appeals have no chance whatever of succeeding. Sometimes they are brought because the claimant cannot believe that the law can be so unfair as to deprive him of his benefit. A commonplace example used to be claims for home confinement grant. An expectant mother would have made all arrangements for a confinement at home, and spent money for it; complications would arise so that she had to be whisked off to hospital at the last minute. In one such case the mother was admitted to the maternity ward shortly before midnight. Five days later, the child having been born, the woman's husband was driving to take her home; his car broke down; there was no Sunday bus service, and she came out the next day. The rigid rule—that she be discharged not later than the end of the fifth day after her admission denied her a claim; had she either been admitted to the hospital five minutes later, or her husband obtained a taxi on the Sunday, she would have been entitled to the full grant. Eventually the law has been changed, I am happy to say. Also, mothers cannot believe that they lose their family allowances after six months' delay, however good their reason for their late presentation of the allowance book. Human problems arise with those who are retired before 65. It may be a bank manager or a company director. These issues are usually about the rule that a person is disqualified for benefit if he refuses to accept a suitable situation. Some cause less difficulty than others. One such 60-year-old claimant informed the Employment Exchange that the job must be from 9.30 to 12.30 on Mondays, Tuesdays and Wednesdays, within one mile of his home in the suburbs and at a salary of at least £30 a week. He appealed to the tribunal when the insurance officer disqualified him in respect of unemployment benefit.

Late claims for various benefits are frequently before the tribunal. Apart from the common total bar after six months, short time limits, but fortunately less short than they used to be, are imposed for all claims unless there is good cause for the delay. The Commissioner has ruled that ignorance of the law is never good cause; most late claim appeals are by persons who have never claimed the benefit before, and did not know either that they were entitled or that they had exceeded the rigid time limit.

It is extraordinary what common fallacies there are about social security claims. For example, dismissed workers often believe that they cannot claim unemployment benefit until their employer hands them their insurance cards. A distressingly large number of married women believe that they qualify for a full pension at 60 if they have the last ten years' contributions on their cards. Of course, not all claimants fall for these fallacies. It is commonly thought that one cannot collect sickness benefit if one is paid by one's firm for sick leave, or that one cannot draw holiday pay and sick pay simultaneously. Yet many local offices find a great increase in sickness claims during the local holiday week.

Claims for family allowances are usually centrally decided by the family allowance headquarters at Newcastle. Their submissions when claimant appeals are expertly prepared, and are usually found legally compelling by local tribunals. These cases often require one to delve deeply into family relationships.

For example, is a claimant maintaining his absent child when he occasionally sends him presents? New problems have arisen in this area with increases in the number of immigrant families. When are marriages in Moslem mosques valid in England? What is the effect of polygamous marriages abroad? One loses family allowances after six months' absence, and the penalty is greater if one is not born in England; what of the Pakistani family who drive their minibus with eight children to Lahore and back and have their return cross-Channel car ferry booked on the last day of the six months, only to find that they cannot land at Dover because of fog? Is it relevant whether the ship was within the three-mile limit before the last day of the six months elapsed?

Frequently difficult legal questions arise. The local office inform the claimant on the appropriate form that he has been granted special hardship allowance for a certain period. In fact it had been granted for a much shorter period, and the letter was a mistake. He relied on it until he was too late to claim. Was the Department estopped by that letter? Frequently a tribunal has to interpret redundancy agreements drawn up at national level in order to estimate the effect of the rule that compensation in lieu of notice disqualifies a claimant from unemployment benefit. These negotiated agreements are often ambiguously drafted, and those who drafted them normally have not had in mind social security implications; sometimes it is difficult to find whether " understandings " between union and management are part of the claimant's contract of employment. For the same reason complex problems of the appropriate period of notice under the Contracts of Employment Act call for decision. In theory these difficulties should have been eased now that legislation requires employers to give employees notices setting out the terms of employment, but in my tribunal experience employers widely disregard those statutory requirements.

Many such cases have an importance beyond the sum immediately at stake because they are test cases. That consideration apart, the amount at stake in cases may range from 5p to over £1,000. Large claims may arise in industrial injury cases or where the Department claims repayment of unemployment benefit on the ground that the claimant had been self-employed while drawing benefit. Claims for repayment are also common with regard to family and dependant's allowances; for example the mother who continues to draw the allowance although her child has started work.

Appeals

Either the claimant or the insurance officer may appeal from the tribunal's decision. Many of these appeals by claimants have no hope of succeeding, but the right is unrestricted. The insurance officer does not appeal on every occasion when he believes the decision wrong. If he thinks that no issue of principle is involved or that it is not necessary to teach the tribunal a lesson (for example, he agrees with the chairman's dissent) he will be content. In any event the regional insurance officer is consulted before an appeal is made by the insurance officer. In fact claimants appeal thirty times as often as insurance officers.

There are no fully reliable statistics about the number of successful appeals on unemployment benefit to local tribunals and to the Commissioner because the published figures do not distinguish between cases where the decision to disqualify is reversed and cases where disqualification is affirmed but a different period imposed. The percentage of successful appeals to local tribunals in family allowance cases is of the order of

8 per cent.—I have explained that all original decisions are made at headquarters. In contrast perhaps a third of industrial injuries benefit appeals succeed. Approximately one in five appeals for other social security benefits is successful. About one in three appeals to the Commissioner succeeds, except for family allowances where the figure is less than one in five.

An assessment of the tribunals

I think that this system of tribunals deserves the high reputation which it enjoys. Social security benefits are very much the main concern of the Department in charge. The Department cares about the tribunals, and is responsive to criticism. For example, the Department in its Notes for Guidance revealed an understandable anxiety lest passages from medical reports might sometimes have a bad psychological effect on a claimant if disclosed to him. It was pointed out to the Department that if such a claimant were not represented, a tribunal which concealed material evidence, though from the best of motives, would be liable to have its decision quashed for failure to give a fair hearing. A 1967 statutory instrument sanctions non-disclosure where it would otherwise be harmful to the claimant's health, and yet it continues to safeguard the claimant's rights. One excellent device is the setting up of a national advisory committee of layman which advises the Minister on the workings of the system and must be consulted about all proposed changes in the laws or procedures.

So much for praise. Minor improvements here and there might be made. As I have explained, Department officials, not the appellate bodies, are responsible for bringing cases to appeal. I have previously stressed the importance of speedy decisions in this class of case. The annual report of the Department of Health and Social Security does not state the average period of delay between even a decision of a local tribunal and the hearing of an appeal by the Commissioners. I believe that the average period between the making of a claim and its final determination by the Commissioner, if it goes so far, is nine months—there is a two- to three-month gap before the local tribunal hears a case. This seems too long to keep needy citizens waiting. I know that delays in the ordinary courts are worse, but one of the best reasons for setting up administrative tribunals is to cut out time-wasting.

A vexed question is legal aid. I have said that very few claimants have a lawyer, even if they are supported by a trade union. Claimants are never entitled to be legally aided. In the majority of cases a lawyer is unnecessary. He is extremely helpful where the factual issues are complex, especially in claims for industrial injury benefit. Many of those claimants are further handicapped by not having obtained the necessary medical evidence which a lawyer would have secured in advance of the hearing. It is also true that claimants are sometimes hopelessly at sea when legal problems are raised. It must be admitted that at present there is no supply of lawyers who are familiar with social security legislation, except in industrial injury claims. No doubt if legal aid were available, specialist lawyers would appear in due course. Is there a case for chairmen and Commissioners being authorised to grant legal aid in cases of exceptional difficulty at modest rates of pay? It might attract a corps of young lawyers, who would become experts in the field, especially those who are now lost to the law because their urge for social service is not satisfied by a profession which they regard as principally serving the moneyed middle classes. Is it self evident that we should spend over 87 per cent. of our funds for legal aid in civil actions on matrimonial proceedings? One might help 10 claimants for social security for the cost of one divorce suit. At the same time the question arises whether claimants might have some financial help in obtaining reports from medical consultants. Other medical aspects cause concern. Is a combination of three laymen and a general practitioner who cannot ask any questions or be asked any, with no oral medical evidence, the best practicable means of deciding complex medical issues?

I have said nothing about precedents. The Act is silent on whether local tribunals are bound to follow decisions of the Commissioner. In practice they do so as of course; and a chairman who systematically disregarded them had his appointment terminated. I am sure that a Commissioner is not bound to follow previous decisions of a Commissioner, so that a local tribunal would not be wasting its time if it followed a Commissioner's decision and yet indicated with reasons why it did so reluctantly. Only about one in two hundred decisions by the Commissioner on national insurance is published. These are the only ones chairmen know about, but insurance officers know of others, and often cite them before local tribunals. Some regional offices have copies of all these numbered but unreported decisions; yet no steps are taken to keep chairmen informed. Twice, early in 1974, an insurance officer appearing before me cited highly relevant unreported decisions of whose existence I was totally, and excusably, unaware. It is particularly disconcerting for a chairman to have his tribunal's decision reversed by the Commissioner because it conflicted with an unreported previous decision of the Commissioner of which both he and the insurance officer were unaware, and still worse to learn that the unreported decision had been considered in an unreported judgment of the Divisional Court of the Queen's Bench Division. The Fisher

Report on Abuse of Social Security Benefits recently reiterated my view that tribunals should have a subpoena power. This would ensure, for instance, production of hospital records and notes. Why the sharp contrast with industrial tribunals where not only is there a power to subpoena documents and witnesses but the President of the National Industrial Relations Court in 1974 laid down that the industrial tribunals had a duty to bring the eixstence of those powers to the notice of litigants? As always, precedent is more of a trap to laymen than to lawyers. Take the case where a claim for a wife's allowance failed if she earned £2·15 a week. She kept lodgers, and it became necessary to estimate her profit. Because in a case 10 years earlier the law had ruled that food would cost £1·25 per head, the insurance officer had assumed that £1·25 was all he could deduct from what each lodger paid her—he believed the precedent precluded asking whether food prices had increased in the subsequent 10 years.

It is common practice for chairmen of many tribunals, such as road transport tribunals and rent assessment committees, to have regular meetings at the appropriate Department. No such meetings are held in the Department of Health and Social Security. Yet chairmen sometimes feel that the law, either in statute or statutory instrument, or in Commissioners' decisions which they must follow, could well be reconsidered. Chairmen have long known that many regulations were incomprehensible, but could do nothing about it. The judges were ignorant of this state of affairs because they never had to interpret them. Now that recent changes in statute confront the judges for the first time with these laws in certain cases before them on appeal, we read for example of Lord Justice Willmer saying in the Court of Appeal of some of these regulations " I regard it as deplorable that in a matter which so vitally affects the lives and welfare of working men, there should be so much obscurity and so much room for doubt."

I regard this last point seriously. We all know how difficult it is to draw up regulations in simple language. Perhaps it does not matter much if only experts will have to interpret them. I submit that social security laws are a special case. They have to be understood by millions of ordinary folk, by trade union officials who try to advise their members, by thousands of civil servants who are not lawyers and by tribunals on which a majority of laymen sit. I maintain that Parliament has a special responsibility here to see that these laws are intelligible to those who use them. In this Parliament has failed completely. This mass of law is obscurely drafted, and what is worse, as each year goes by, it becomes harder to understand. I believe that the government owes it to citizens to redraft these Acts and regulations completely, so that those who understand plain English will, on reading them, understand what their rights are.

Let me give a few examples of the effect of the present laws. A corporation employs park-keepers full time in the summer and at weekends in the winter. The first winter a park-keeper will be paid unemployment benefit for the days on which he does not work. When his second summer ends he is amazed to find that his claim for unemployment benefit is rejected; the Commissioner has held that he is not ordinarily employed on those days in his employment. Take the somewhat similar case of the professional musician who teaches music part-time for the local education authority. If he works every Tuesday and Wednesday only, he will draw no benefit. It did not occur to him to ask the authoritity to employ him on different days each week. Special hardship allowance claims give rise to controversy. Consider the case where the industrial injury had reduced the victim's ability to earn bonus by several pounds a week. Skilled labour at his trade was so scarce that his job was not in jeopardy; previous decisions compelled a rejection of the claim for special hardship allowance because he could pursue his regular occupation. Had he been compelled to take on another job where his earnings exceeded his present earnings he would have had a claim. It is also interesting to consider how the Department endeavours to find out how much an injured person could earn in another employment. The Department tells the Department of Employment and Productivity what are the relevant characteristics of the claimant and his disabilities. The Department of Employment and Productivity replies that the claimant might work in a certain occupation and earn so much. It often happens that the claimant has not known that the insurance officer has made this inquiry until he is notified of the date of his appeal. He had never been told that he was considered suitable for a certain job, he was not registered for it at the employment exchange, and had never been offered any such job. It may be that the insurance officer, who does not see the claimant, is acting reasonably in contacting the Department of Employment and Productivity in this way before making his initial decision. It seems strange, however, that the insurance officer will continue to rely on this written evidence before the local tribunal in order to justify his rejection of the special hardship allowance. It is difficult to see why a report by someone who has never seen a claimant, that he is suitable for a job which has never been offered, and a job of whose availability he is totally unaware, and where there is no evidence that there are any vacancies in the job, still less that the claimant could successfully apply for one, can be regarded as cogent evidence.

Claimants, and certainly many lay members of tribunals, are disturbed by the rigidity of social security laws. An allowance is lost altogether if earnings exceed a certain figure after deductions. If the excess is threepence it is never possible to make the allowance less threepence. No doubt the Department has a powerful argument in saying that rules must be definite and that the administrative expense of making proportionate awards would be too great. For example, a man was paying £2·50 a week to his wife under a court order. When he was sick he drew £2·50 additional sickness benefit for his dependent wife. Later dependant's benefit was increased to £2·80. Next time he was sick he was refused dependant's benefit altogether because the £2·50 he was paying on the court order was less than the £2·80. If he had known his rights he could have voluntarily paid her 30p more and so have been £2·50 better off. There are similar anxieties about the fact that claims are absolutely barred after six months. A claimant may inquire at the local office whether she has a claim; she is wrongly told that she has no claim, so that she never completes a form. Seven months later she discovers that she had a claim. The tribunal must dismiss her appeal. As one recalls that it is very doubtful whether a claimant would recover damages in negligence against a Department for wrongful advice on a possible claim against funds administered by them, when she was not precluded from making the claim at the time, there is sympathy with the claimant in her plight.

I hope that I have shown that national insurance tribunals work well. A zealous well-managed government department can work with lay, lawyer and medical members of tribunals in such a way as to dispense justice within the Welfare State. The law has made a valuable and original contribution to making our system of social security work fairly. Britain devised an entirely new legal system for the problem. The original scheme was a good one, the machinery to see to its operation and improvement has worked well. Changes have been made where necessary. And the cheapness of the system is astonishing—the overhead expenses are less than 10 per cent. of the benefits distributed. It provides an excellent example of the resourcefulness of our jurisprudence. Not the least of its virtues is that the citizen plays such an important part both as adviser and decision-maker.

Chapter 2

RENT AND NATIONAL HEALTH SERVICE TRIBUNALS

In my last lecture I examined social security tribunals at length. Tonight I begin by looking at another set of tribunals with markedly different powers and structure. These are the furnished houses rent tribunals and the rent assessment committees, which are supervised by the Department of the Environment.

Rent Control

Rents of unfurnished houses had been subject to rent control since the early 1920s. Even as late as the end of the 1939–45 war there were no similar controls over furnished accommodation. A government committee on rent control known as the Ridley Committee reported in 1945 in favour of setting up special tribunals in order to prevent profiteering in the expected post-war housing shortage. Following on that report, the Furnished Houses (Rent Control) Act 1946 was passed.

The early days of rent tribunals

The tribunals were to determine the rents of only those houses or parts of houses whose tenants referred them to the tribunals. The efficacy of this scheme of rent control depended on the use made of the tribunals by tenants. The government was therefore concerned to induce tenants to use them. It believed that tenants of furnished accommodation would dread going to the ordinary courts. For the same reason it decided to make the tribunals as informal as possible. It did not even require the chairman to be a lawyer. Whereas regulations made under social security legislation have (as we saw) to be considered by a body of laymen known as the national insurance advisory committee (which exercises a very close supervision), and thereafter have to be laid before Parliament, the Secretary of State for the Environment is empowered to make regulations under the Rent Act without even having to lay them at all before Parliament. The government was manifestly determined throughout to resist pressure to have the proceedings formalised.

In the early days many of these tribunals behaved in a very informal manner indeed; sometimes only two members would sit, although the Act required three. Powerful interest groups were naturally hostile to the tribunals—after all the tribunals would be reducing rents charged by landlords. Owners were not slow to challenge in the ordinary courts the legality of what the tribunals were doing, and the Divisional Court of the King's Bench Division viewed them with unconcealed disfavour and distrust and kept them on as tight a rein as possible. Subsequent governments have greatly improved the system. Lawyers only are now appointed as chairmen, and their appointment has to be approved by the Lord Chancellor. The courts now seldom interfere with their decisions, and when they do, a chairman, on whose conduct they comment unfavourably, is unlikely to have his appointment renewed. I will now explain the practical working of these tribunals.

The tribunal consists of three members, who are appointed for periods of about a year at a time, but who are ordinarily reappointed. There is also a panel of reserve members who act during a member's incapacity or absence. One member is appointed chairman and another reserve chairman. The tribunal appoints its clerk, who is ordinarily a civil servant in the Department of the Environment. This means that the tribunal has full control over the organisation of its sittings. If it is not disposing of cases promptly the fault lies squarely with the tribunal and its clerk. Tenants make written applications to the tribunal, the clerk notifies the landlord and seeks to collect further information from both parties on forms in standard use. After giving at least seven days' notice to landlord and tenant, the tribunal should arrange hearings so that it will dispose of an application as soon as it has assembled the information and passed it on to the parties. Tribunals view the premises both inside and out, by appointment, and normally hold an oral hearing later the same day; it is convenient to dispose of three or four cases in one day by inspecting in the morning and holding hearings in the afternoon. The Press and public may attend hearings. In the majority of cases both landlord and tenant also attend, although the tribunal is allowed to decide the reference in the absence of one or both parties on proof that they have been duly notified of the hearing.

Functions

The main work of the tribunal is to hear applications by tenants for the reduction of rent and for the grant of security of tenure. Where the rent has previously been fixed, either party may in addition ask the tribunal to revise it in view of change of circumstances since it was originally determined. A landlord may also ask the tribunal to reduce a period of security of tenure which it has previously granted, on the ground that the tenant has subsequently broken the terms of his contract, or has been guilty of conduct which is a nuisance or annoyance to adjoining occupiers, or has used the dwelling for an illegal or immoral purpose, or that the condition of the dwelling has deteriorated owing to some act or neglect on his part, or that the condition of any furniture has deteriorated owing to ill-treatment by him or anyone residing or lodging with him.

Legal problems of jurisdiction

The framers of the 1946 Act wrongly assumed that the task of the tribunal is merely to fix rents, so that lawyers would be superfluous, and the proceedings need bear little resemblance to judicial hearings. The work of the tribunal teems with legal problems. Its first task is always to decide whether it has jurisdiction. Has the contract been properly referred to the tribunal? Only a party may refer a contract. In this class of case it is often very difficult to decide who are the parties. There is a written agreement in perhaps one case in a hundred. The Landlord and Tenant Act 1962 imposes on landlords who let houses on weekly tenancies (but on no others) a duty to provide rent books, which must contain the name and address of the landlord and particulars of the rent and of the terms and conditions of the contract. Perhaps about one weekly tenancy in two referred to the tribunal has a rent book of any kind, and perhaps about one in a hundred has a rent book in which the landlord has recorded the required particulars. No attempt is made by the police, local authorities or anybody else to enforce the law against landlords—one notices that enforcement of the criminal law against landlords is usually half-hearted. The Act authorises local authorities to prosecute for these offences, but they plainly make no serious attempt to execute this responsibility efficiently. Typical difficulties are where a landlord has let a flat to some nurses whose names appear in the rent book and then one or more of these nurses leaves the flat and others move in. Is there now a contract by the landlord with the surviving nurse and the newcomers jointly? When is one person effectively referring a contract to a tribunal as agent for the tenant or tenants? When a contract has been validly referred, the Act provides that if " before the tribunal have entered upon consideration of the reference," it is withdrawn, the tribunal has no jurisdiction. When has a tribunal so entered upon consideration? Only at the hearing, or when it requests written information from the landlord and notifies him of the hearing, or when it commences to inspect, and what if half way through the inspection the tenant intimates that he wants to drop the action? What is the tribunal to do if, as sometimes happens, it has evidence that the withdrawal was procured by coercion or fraudulent misrepresentation on the part of the landlord?

The next problem is to decide whether there is a contract within the Act. Formal leases are virtually unknown, so that the inquiry is difficult. The owner may argue that he has granted the applicant the right merely to sleep in one of the beds in one of his rooms. The applicant may reply that the occupants share the exclusive occupation of the room or that each has the exclusive occupation of the bed and its surrounding floor space. It is certainly not enough to decide whether applicants are lodgers. Until 1966, if the applicant had exclusive occupation and was paying rent in part for furniture or services, the tribunal had jurisdiction. It was enough if the proportion of the rent represented by the furniture and services amounted to something more than *de minimis*, say 5 per cent. The effect of the Rent Act 1968 is that the tribunal has jurisdiction only if the proportion of the furniture's value—the value of the services no longer counts—to the total rent is such as to take the contract outside the former Rent and Mortgage Interest Restrictions Acts 1920 to 1939. Those Acts do not define what that proportion must be. Until 1974 there was total uncertainty on the part of tribunals on how they were to interpret this. Some had assumed that accommodation was furnished if the tenant was provided with necessary furniture: bed, chairs, table and the like, others thought that the furniture had to represent some percentage of the rent, say 10 per cent. or 15 per cent. or 20 per cent. This issue was clarified by *Woodward* v. *Docherty*, a decision of the Court of Appeal in 1974.[1] The court held that a flat was not " furnished " simply because the landlord provided fully adequate furniture. The tribunal had to decide the rental value of the furniture at the beginning of that tenancy, and would arrive at that figure through first deciding how much it would have cost the landlord to buy it. The court was not called on to decide what percentage was required, but it is probable that the effect of the decision is that a flat is not " furnished " unless the proportion of the rental value of the furniture to the total rent charged is of the order of 15 per cent. to 20 per cent. The consequences of this ruling will sometimes be odd. Suppose the furniture to be calculated to be worth £2 a week, in each of three identical flats. In flat A the landlord provides no services and charges £8 a week; the flat is " furnished." In flat B the landlord provides electricity for lighting, heating and cooking, so that the rent is £14 a week; the flat is " unfurnished." Flat C—everything is the same as in flat A except that the contract rent is £14 a week; the flat is now " unfurnished."

All tribunal chairmen have to become experts on the law relating to notice to quit. If say a notice to quit served by the landlord on the tenant became operative the day before

---

[1] [1974] 1 W.L.R. 966.

the tenant referred the contract to the tribunal, the tribunal would have no jurisdiction. In perhaps a half of the cases referred to the tribunal a notice to quit has been served. The judges used to hold that notices to determine weekly tenancies had to give 28 days' *clear* notice—a notice given on a Friday to expire four Fridays later was void. When that was the law—Lord Parker, the Lord Chief Justice, decided in 1966 that the 28 days' notice need no longer be clear—a tribunal might find about 75 per cent. of notices to quit void. The proportion of void notices is still high, even after that simplification of the law. Many landlords have not adjusted themselves to the fact that for the last 18 years four weeks' and not one week's notice has been required. Trouble also arises from the requirement that the notice must become effective on a day when a period of the tenancy ends. When there is no adequate rent book it is difficult to ascertain the day of the week on which the tenancy begins. It is of course perfectly straightforward to draft the notice to meet this contingency of not knowing the exact rent day, by making the notice to quit become effective on a fixed date at least 28 days after service or on the next day afterwards when that current week of the tenancy shall end. Unfortunately the printed form of one of the law stationers on which many landlords and their solicitors rely has not in this respect been altered in the way that the 1957 Act made necessary, so that many notices to quit on their forms continue to be void. And what is a good notice for a weekly tenancy may prove equally useless because it later emerges that the rent was paid monthly on a monthly tenancy. Even if the period of a valid notice to quit has expired, further difficulties arise when the landlord continues to receive payments from the tenant after that date, for the tenant may contend that the tribunal still has jurisdiction because he remains in occupation by virtue of a contract in consideration of the payment of rent.

The contract of tenancy

When the tribunal is satisfied that it has jurisdiction it must next find out what are the terms of the contract. This is usually difficult, particularly with regard to furniture. Not once in a hundred cases is there an inventory. Sometimes a tenant does not want all the furniture made available to him by the landlord, so that either the landlord removes it, or the tenant later puts some of it in the cellar because he says that it is unusable. The landlord may maintain that not all the furniture provided is still there because the tenant has saved money on coal by burning the landlord's furniture instead. Services too create a problem. For how many hours a week is hot water provided? Does the landlord provide a window cleaner, or someone to clean the shared bathroom and staircase? More difficult, is an electricity sub-meter calibrated by the landlord within the limits of the maximum charge permitted by local orders made under the Electricity Acts? This kind of legislation and the inescapable obligations of landlords under housing legislation have to be at the tribunal's fingertips. When a facility is available but not used, was its provision part of the contract? Facilities for car parking or the installation of a telephone in the hall are illustrations. When the tribunal is inspecting, it often sees notices in the premises which purport to regulate the conduct of the tenants. Those of the " Please clean the bath after using " type occasion no difficulty of course. " No pets," " No visitors after 11 p.m.," " No washing clothes in bathroom," " No guitars," and the like are more germane.

Determining the rent

Not until all these often complex issues have been resolved can the tribunal begin what most would think of as its only task: namely, determining the reasonable rent. The Act gives no guidance on how to do that. The Act does not even require any members to view the flat, but as I have said it is the invariable practice of members to inspect both inside and outside. The tribunal has to decide what is the reasonable rent in respect of the particular contract of tenancy. It is obviously not enough to decide what is the rental value of the accommodation alone. Suppose the tribunal is agreed on the rental value of the premises, it may be presented with problems like this. How much do you deduct if no guests may visit without previous permission, or if they must leave by 10 p.m. or if there is a notice that visiting hours are restricted to three afternoons a week from 2 p.m. to 4 p.m.? Or if the tenant is forbidden to operate a radio? Or to have a cat or children? Or is required to keep clean the bathroom and passages, although he has only a bed-sitter and is not provided by the landlord with a vacuum cleaner? Or has to allow access at all times to his rooms for other tenants so that they can take refuse to the bin behind the house? Or is forbidden to launder or to dry laundry? Or is required to repair a leaking roof or to decorate throughout before he may begin the tenancy? Or take the now common provision in student lettings that the rent will be reduced in vacations and be a mere holding rent during the summer provided that tenants are not actually residing in the premises?

Tribunals use various methods to determine the rent. Almost all use some mathematical calculation at least as a guide. They may ascertain the gross rateable value of the house and estimate what proportion the letting bears to the whole of the house—perhaps most contracts are in respect of parts of a house which are not separately rated. In order to arrive at the letting value of the flat premises, they multiply this figure by some numerical factor of their own choice. They calculate the cost of the services to the landlord, and after allowing him a profit on them, add that to the figure they have arrived at for the flat itself. A profit must also be allowed for the furniture, and this is normally arrived at by estimating its capital value and awarding a percentage of that, which might be in the range of 15 to 40 per cent. per annum. Some tribunals ignore the rateable value, and make their initial calculation by estimating the capital value of the unit with vacant possession and awarding a percentage of that, which might be at least 12 per cent. Some tribunals will first, in the light of their inspection, assess the rental value of the accommodation as if it were unfurnished, and then make the other additions. Before finally reaching its decision the tribunal will make sure that the final figure is reasonable in the light of its store of accumulated knowledge about comparable rents in the area.

Security of tenure

In addition to determining the rent, the tribunal has to decide whether to postpone the coming into force of a notice to quit, if a valid one had been served and had not become operative when the matter was first referred to the tribunal. If the tenancy had already been determined there would be no jurisdiction. If the notice to quit is invalid or if none has been served the tribunal may still grant security of tenure. The maximum period allowed is six months, but the period may be renewed on application, up to six months at a time. One of the curiosities of the Act (until amended by the 1974

Act) was that if no valid notice to quit had been served, then, if the tribunal granted less than six months' security, no subsequent renewal was possible, whereas, if there was a notice to quit, an extension was allowed however short the initial period of security granted had been. The paradox was that a solicitor might often strenuously argue in front of the tribunal that his client's notice to quit was valid, when he would have curtailed the tribunal's freedom to grant security had he had the acumen to admit that the notice was void. It is entirely in the discretion of the tribunal how much security to give. At hearings more time is usually spent on this issue than on evidence about the rent. Obviously, the behaviour of tenant and landlord is relevant, in particular whether the tenant pays the rent promptly. The tribunal has also to balance the need of the tenant for the accommodation (and his ability to obtain alternative premises) against any claim for vacant possession by the landlord, who may wish to sell the property with vacant possession, or to live there with his family. Tribunals conduct hearings in as informal a manner as possible and allow hearsay evidence. They normally announce their decision immediately after arriving at it. They are under no obligation to give reasons unless " requested on or before the giving or notification of the decision." Such requests are seldom made, but the Department has wisely expressed the hope that tribunals will give reasons.

Judicial review

There is no appeal from the decision of rent tribunals to any higher administrative tribunal. Appeal lies on points of law to the Divisional Court of the Queen's Bench Division. That court can also quash on an order of certiorari (I will say more about that later) any decision arrived at without jurisdiction, or in breach of the rules of natural justice or obtained by fraud, or having error of law on the face of the record. The county court is empowered to determine whether a rent tribunal has jurisdiction. The difference between an administrative appeal and review by the ordinary courts, even the county court, is illustrated when I tell you that many rent tribunals have never been challenged in the courts. Had there been an appeal to an administrative tribunal from a rent tribunal I am sure that challenges would have been very much more frequent.

Why a tenant goes to the tribunal

So far I have merely stated in a descriptive way what rent tribunals do. You (and the Hamlyn trustees) no doubt expect my own views on them: I must try not to disappoint you. First let me say that no more than one tenant in three brings his case because he thinks that his rent is too high. Of that third a quarter come, not because they want to, but because officials of the Supplementary Benefits Commission warn them that they think their rents too high and lead them to believe that they will reduce their benefits unless they refer their rents to the tribunal. The Commission could not itself refer the cases because local authorities are the only bodies other than tenants allowed to refer cases. This is a gap in the Act because the Supplementary Benefits Commission has no power to make tenants go to the tribunal—many of their clients resist the pressure, the amount of which varies tremendously from locality to locality. Why is the Department of the Environment opposed to giving the power to the Supplementary Benefits Commission? Surely not because of some irrelevant convention that one department must not meddle in the affairs of another. And why is it that, when local authorities do take a case, they are not even entitled to be told about the hearing? The tenant has to fend for himself. Many tenants know that they are being overcharged, but fear the consequences if they complain to the tribunal. They either do not know that the law protects them against harassment and eviction, or simply have no confidence in the law's protection. Local authorities take no steps to inform the tenants that they have been given the power precisely to avoid tenants themselves being involved. My inquiries suggest that local councillors are unaware that they have the power. It is significant that so small a proportion of cases is referred voluntarily by tenants because they think that the rent is too high.

What is perhaps even more striking is that about one in three of the tenants who do complain about their rents withdraw their applications before the tribunal can adjudicate. What often happens is that landlords go to great lengths to keep cases from the tribunal: they don't want other tenants to find out about overcharging, and they don't want them to get security. The Act is powerless to protect the tenant against this folly. The landlord can promise a reduction in rent on condition that the tenant withdraws his application, but there is then nothing to prevent him from serving a notice to quit on the tenant and afterwards charging his successor whatever rent he likes. Many landlords of numerous flats have a policy of trying at all costs to buy off tenants who refer their rents to the tribunal. Their policy rests solely on economic grounds: it is cheaper to offer large reductions to the occasional dissatisfied tenant than to run the risk of other tenants reading reports in the Press of an order for reduction of rent and then seeking similar reductions themselves.

Some defects in the system

The Act prohibits a tribunal from determining a reasonable rent if the tenant has withdrawn his application before the tribunal entered upon consideration of the case. There should be machinery whereby the tribunal could investigate the circumstances surrounding a withdrawal and, if it thought fit, determine the maximum rent. As matters are, we reach the startling conclusion that out of every six cases referred to the tribunal it hears only one that was brought to it because the tenant was complaining about the rent.

Most tenants go to a tribunal because they are seeking security of tenure. The landlord has served them with a notice to quit or has threatened to do so, or seems likely to evict them by force. That of course does not mean that their rent is not too high, for many tenants are so glad to find any accommodation at all that they will not argue about the rent. Still less does it mean that the tenant is a bad one; he may have had the temerity to have demanded a rent book or to have reported the state of repair to the public health department. Some tenants come to the tribunal as a retaliatory measure against the landlord. They owe rent and suspect that his forbearance has come to an end, so that they will have to leave; their parting shot is to try and cut down the rent which he can charge to new tenants, or, pending the hearing, to obtain a few weeks' grace in which they will pay no rent.

Many tenants come to the rent tribunal because they find living conditions intolerable. Landlords cut off gas and electricity supplies, or allow unendurable stench to persist in the cellar, or fail to repair gaping holes in the roof so that tenants have to put buckets on the floor to collect the rain. The duty of the tribunal is to determine what is the reasonable rent payable under the contract. The absurd result is that the tribunal has to ignore the failure of the landlord to carry out his obligations. Of course the legalistic answer is that the tenant has his remedy for breach of contract in the county court. For this class of tenant that remedy is useless and illusory. It would take him at least a month to obtain a legal aid certificate, and perhaps an average of another three months before the county court could hear his claim. Very useful for a tenant of this type who normally moves house at least every year. I am convinced that the machinery of civil judicial administration is completely failing to do justice for furnished tenants in houses in multiple occupation. There is a parallel situation in employer-employee relations. Those who serve on national insurance and industrial tribunals know that cases of unlawful dismissal abound without legal redress simply because the ineffective county court, and not tribunals seized of other aspects of the problem such as redundancy, alone has jurisdiction, because the Industrial Relations Act 1974 has repealed the enabling provision of the Industrial Relations Act 1971 which would have given jurisdiction to the tribunals. Here, and on consumer complaints, we could profitably look at the Race Relations Act conciliation machinery. Tribunals should be empowered to reduce the rent when a landlord is not performing his obligations. A landlord would be able to have the rent revised on proof that the obligation was again being performed. I am well aware that local authorities have powers under housing and public health legislation to enforce certain standards of repair and provision of essential services, but it is a matter of everyday experience that local authorities have not the staff to carry out these functions effectively. The experienced landlord can cock a snook at public health officers for a long time.

Another similar defect arises with regard to the demanding of premiums by landlords. Key money, estate agents charging tenants with commission, possibly the landlord's solicitors making tenants pay for the costs of tenancy agreements, tenants having to deposit money with the landlord as security for not damaging the flat and so on, are all illegal. Yet I suppose in one in ten cases before a tribunal illegal premiums have been extorted, often by agreements drawn up by the landlord's solicitors. The tribunal has no power in the case of these furnished lettings to order repayment of the illegal premiums, and the tenant would act unlawfully if he deducted the premium from his rent. Why should criminal conduct be condoned in this way?

Rental changes are to date from the decision of the tribunal. Greater justice would be done if the reduction (or increase on a reconsideration) could be back-dated from the date of reference. It frequently happens that a landlord seeks an adjournment for perfectly good reasons: for example, he or his solicitor are on holiday. The tribunal is empowered to grant an adjournment, but is not expressly authorised to attach conditions, such as that any reduction in rent should be back-dated. This question has another aspect. The landlord must be given an opportunity to make a written return to the tenant's application. In practice it is often very difficult to ensure that a landlord who has not replied has received notice of hearing. A tribunal is understandably reluctant then to proceed in his absence; yet any delay in holding the hearing might prejudice the tenant. It should be enacted that the landlord has been duly served whenever notice has been sent to his address as stated in the rent book, and that, whenever there is no rent book or no such address in it, a letter addressed to him at the tenanted premises is adequate notice.

It often happens that tenants refer rents which the tribunal finds to have been previously fixed at a rent lower than the one the landlord is requiring them to pay. It is difficult in practice for tribunals to keep accurate checks of this in houses in multiple occupation, especially when the Department's circulars advise the destruction of old files—the document on which rents are registered with the local authority often does not make it possible to identify the unit let because Parliament made the mistake of not providing for simple house plans (which would identify the various flats in each house) to be attached to the registration document. As one would expect the Act recognises the right of tenants to be repaid that money in excess of the authorised rent received by the landlord. The landlord who charges this excessive rent commits a criminal offence, and the criminal court is authorised also to order the repayment to the tenant of the rents unlawfully demanded and received. But the tenant is prohibited from bringing those criminal proceedings; only the local authority can. In practice most local authorities refuse to prosecute. Some landlords soon realise this and defy the law by continuing to charge illegal higher rents. It is difficult to see why both the police and the tenant, and, indeed where appropriate, the Supplementary Benefits Commission, should be precluded from prosecuting with a view to enforcing the repayment.

The tribunal is often in difficulties with regard to the exercise of its power to grant security. It may regard the rent charged as too low and yet believe the tenant to be in need of protection. A tribunal was prohibited (until the coming into force of the Rent Act 1974) from raising the rent to a level higher than the one charged, so that, if it were to grant security, it would condemn the landlord to receive a rent for that period of protection less than what it finds reasonable.

When circumstances have changed since a rent was fixed, either party may ask the tribunal to reconsider the rent on that account. Obviously, if there is an increase in the cost of supplying electricity, that should be reflected in the authorised rent. A harder question is whether inflation itself is a " change of circumstances." Sometimes the landlord is found to be no longer properly carrying out his obligations to provide services or to maintain the premises; the tribunal cannot reduce the rent for that reason.

Further snags arose after the Rent Act 1965 established rent officers and rent assessment committees to determine the rents of certain unfurnished houses and flats. (The big changes made by the Rent Act 1974 are set out later.) Tenants under those lettings enjoy security of tenure without special grant of it by the authorised tribunal; it is automatic. I have referred already to the difficulty since 1965 of deciding whether a letting was " furnished." It frequently happens that an aggrieved tenant does not know, and cannot be expected to know, the answer. Suppose that he goes to the rent officer. The rent officer is himself uncertain, and allows months to elapse while making inquiries of an unco-operative landlord, before deciding that he had no jurisdiction because the letting was furnished. There is nothing to stop the landlord serving a notice to quit on the tenant meanwhile, so that by the time the rent officer has decided that the tenant should have gone, not to him, but to the furnished rent tribunal, the landlord has effectively determined the tenancy and also deprived the rent tribunal of jurisdiction. It can happen that the rent officer holds the tenancy to be furnished and outside his jurisdiction, and the tribunal holds it to be unfurnished and outside its jurisdiction: nobody will help the tenant. Confusion can arise in another way. A tribunal may have lawfully fixed the rent of a furnished flat before 1965. After 1965 the landlord asks the tribunal to increase it because of changed circumstances. If the amount of furniture in the original letting is not substantial enough to give jurisdiction to the rent tribunal under the Act of 1965 (now 1968) the tribunal would be required to say: "We lawfully fixed the rent before but we have no jurisdiction to alter it now."

Legal aid

Both tribunals, but especially assessment committees, have serious drawbacks. The typical landlord of an unfurnished flat who appeals to a rent assessment committee will be a wealthy property company. Opposed to him will be a tenant on a modest income. The landlord will come, armed not merely with high quality legal advice, but more important, with one or more experts in valuation. For the tenant to have comparable help might cost him 50 pounds a day. Even if the aggrieved tenant were to win, he would still have to meet that expense himself. My inquiries confirm what you would have expected—that not one tenant in a hundred has the help of expert witnesses. The inability of the tenant to pay for those services handicaps him greatly. The praiseworthy unofficial efforts of the Chartered Land Societies' Committee to provide help for needy tenants has not filled the gap which Parliament has left.

The Department of the Environment

Although rent control must inevitably be a small part of the concern of so large a department as the Department of the Environment—it occupies less than one per cent. of the space in its Annual Report—that is not to say that the Department has not advised tribunals. I gave one illustration of this earlier with regard to the definition of furnished premises. Another interesting example was publicised in correspondence in *The Times* in the summer of 1966. The furnished tribunals had always taken account of the supply and demand of houses in carrying out their obligations under the 1946 Act to fix such rent as they thought reasonable in the circumstances. The Rent Act 1965 required rent officers and rent assessment committees, when determining the rents of unfurnished flats, to assume that the number of persons seeking to become tenants of similar houses in the locality is not substantially greater than the number of such houses available for letting, *i.e.* to exclude scarcity value. The Ministry wrote to all chairmen of rent tribunals that it considered that " the rent tribunal may exclude this scarcity value in considering what sum would in all the circumstances be reasonable for a furnished letting." It also appeared to say that if any tenant had permanently improved the letting that permanent improvement was to be disregarded—to disregard it would also be a change of practice. This example raises two questions. First, whether the method of fixing a rent can be treated as changed by a later statute which makes no reference to the power in the earlier Act. Secondly, whether the Department have given secret advice to rent tribunals on difficult and contested points of interpretation of the Acts under which they work. This is of course an entirely different question from the issuing of circulars which summarise Acts or draw attention to recent decisions under the Act. The letter writer in *The Times* strongly criticised the Ministry's action.

I have stressed before how important speed is in this area. If there is to be a gap of nine months between reference to a rent officer and decision by a rent assessment committee I would argue this is inexcusable—yet delays in London have greatly exceeded that period.

No requirements as to qualification for membership of either rent tribunals or rent assessment committees are laid down. It is the normal practice for the president of the assessment committee to see to it that both a valuer and a lawyer sit on each panel: this is wise. The ideal combination on rent tribunals is a lawyer, a valuer and a woman member with experience of social conditions in working-class accommodation.

The requirements about registering rents with the local authority are unsatisfactory. They do not enable an inquirer to ascertain the details of the contract of tenancy. They do not set out any of the conditions of the contract. On the other hand they are required to contain prejudicial and irrelevant material. I refer particularly to the name of the tenant. Some landlords keep lists from the register of those tenants who apply to tribunals and will not accept any of them as their tenants.

The procedures of both the tribunals and the committees are not prescribed in detail by law. When the committees were first set up, an unofficial practice grew up under ministerial encouragement whereby everybody copied what Sir Sidney Littlewood's London committee did. This led to such absurd situations as the committee inspecting the outside but not the inside of premises. Of course such rules were soon found to be so unworkable that they had to be withdrawn. Other tribunals achieve fair results by subjecting their procedures to the rule of law; Parliament should have done the same with rent control.

You may think that there is still much more to criticise about tribunals in this field than there is in those connected with social security. You may ask whether it is significant that the approach of the Department of the Environment is different. There are neither national nor local advisory committees to oversee the working of the legislation, which occupies a minor place in a large and busy Department. Rent tribunal chairmen never meet and are never consulted *en masse* by the Department. Especially it is doubtful whether the Department was wise to decide not to integrate in the Rent Act 1965 machinery for controlling furnished and unfurnished accommodation. The system of appointing regional presidents under the Rent Act 1968 with an oversight of both rent assessment committees and rent tribunals has brought about an improvement in co-ordination at regional level.

Rent Act 1974

The Rent Act 1974 has transferred from rent tribunals to rent officers and rent assessment committees much of the jurisdiction relating to furnished dwellings. The most important category of jurisdiction retained by rent tribunals is where the dwelling forms part of a building and that building is not a purpose-built block of flats and the landlord occupies as his residence another part of the building. For the first time they are also given jurisdiction over such dwellings even though they are unfurnished. The difficulties of defining "furnished" will remain for residential-landlord tenancies created before the 1974 Act; only if they are "unfurnished" within the *Woodward* v. *Docherty* rule will they retain that security of tenure enjoyed before 1974 as regulated tenancies within Part IV of the Rent Act 1968. The 1974 Act leaves unchanged the constitution and procedures of rent tribunals.

It shows signs of ill-considered drafting which will lead to difficulties in practice. For example, to dispense with the former necessity for a landlord who had to pay a rate increase to apply to a tribunal for an increase in the registered rent the Act provides for separate registration of rent and rates. But the vast majority of rent tribunal cases will be ones where there is no separate assessment of the flat. How then is the landlord to be kept to his proportionate allowance for rate increases when the register does not indicate what proportion of the whole house the tribunal applied to this unit as the basis of its rent fixing?

I want to hark back at this stage to a matter which I touched on in my previous lecture. Most lower-income group families live in tenanted accommodation. Legal problems affecting tenancies concern those tenants more intimately than any other branch of the law. A satisfactory legal system would have a clear-cut set of rules which were enforced cheaply and effectively. It would be plain what a landlord's obligations are and the due performance of those duties would be ensured. Ours meets none of those requirements, and I am deeply disturbed about it. The legal rules themselves are confused. Some powers of enforcement are in the hands of tenants, and others in the hands of local authorities. Unpunished and even undetected violations of the laws are widespread. The county court, with its delays and forbidding forms and formalities, is an inappropriate agency for the unaided aggrieved tenant—he simply turns his back on the county court. The poor have nobody to go to for advice—the law is so complex that the Citizens' Advice Bureaux cannot cope. There is no specialist legal talent available for the poor in this branch of the law. Even if there were, the law itself cannot provide speedy justice. Existing tribunals should be empowered to adjust rents when leasing obligations are contravened. A special corps of lawyers should be available to help the poor in these and related problems of the Welfare State. The tax, company and town planning problems of the affluent are more than adequately handled by specialist lawyers. The legal profession provides no comparable service for the equally pressing problems of the poor in the Welfare State. I am not convinced that we should go on spending 80 per cent. to 90 per cent. of our legal aid funds on matrimonial proceedings and spend not a halfpennny on assistance before Welfare State tribunals.

The Future of Social Security and Rent Tribunals

I make no apology for having talked at length about these tribunals. I have done so for several reasons. This kind of examination of these or other tribunals has never been made. Unless it is carried out neither the Department responsible nor the public know how our tribunals are faring. It proves also that much could be done to improve these arrangements. There is room for change both in the organisation of the tribunals and in the laws which they dispense. At the moment there is no machinery for unearthing these defects and no procedure for curing them. It is of course true that the position is no worse than with the courts. That does not console me in the least. We know that the machinery of the courts has needed overhauling for a long time—no professional is taken in by the flattering remarks inevitably made about our courts by legal practitioners during after-dinner speeches at lawyers' dinners. In my view the Welfare State has failed unless it takes heed of the shortcomings of the ordinary courts. After all, as

I have tried to show in my previous lecture, administrative tribunals were set up under the Welfare State because the ordinary courts were not trusted to carry out the new tasks properly.

You may feel that I should not generalise about administrative tribunals on the strength of two kinds. I have talked at length to chairmen of other kinds of tribunal. Their experience merely reinforces mine; that there are defects in administration and in the substantive law for the removal of which no arrangements are made. I have also made a point of making spot checks of other kinds of tribunal. I found none of them completely satisfactory. I agree with the general opinion that supplementary benefit tribunals need improvement. What is quite certain is that the two which I have dealt with at length are far better than many other types.

National Health Service Tribunals

Take the tribunals set up under the National Health Service for example. Their task is to ensure that doctors, dentists and other practitioners are carrying out their obligations under the scheme, and to deal with those who are thought to be wanting. One might have been forgiven for thinking that this involved equally two classes of persons: affected practitioners and aggrieved patients. Nothing of the kind. A wholly unsatisfactory structure of tribunals has been set up, simply because the Ministry of Health gave the practitioners what the B.M.A. and other pressure groups insisted on as the price of accepting the National Health Service. What is at stake is not whether a practitioner shall be removed from his professional register, but at most whether he shall be allowed to practise under the National Health Service. Yet five different bodies have to consider and make a decision before a practitioner is taken off that list against his will.

Not even at the first stages of his complaint is the patient allowed to hire the help of a lawyer, whereas of course the practitioner will have available the expert help of a representative of his defence union. Pressure was put on the Ministry of Health to allow their officials to help claimants with their cases; the Ministry refused. In 1974 Parliament even removed the right of a patient to be represented by an unpaid lawyer friend. Only when lawyer M.P.s realised that might stop them from wooing their constituents by helping them was the *status quo* restored by amending statutory instrument. The clerks to some local executive councils obstruct patients who have a complaint by refusing to let them have copies of prescription forms or medical reports, and the patients can do nothing about it. No member of the public or Press is allowed to be present to see that justice is done. Even when the local executive councils uphold the citizen's complaint, the practitioner's identity is never revealed.

If the citizen is aggrieved at the failure to punish the guilty practitioner adequately he has no appeal; the practitioner may always appeal against his punishment even if he admits his guilt. If the case goes all the way to the central hearing appellate body, the National Health Service Tribunal, it is heard in private unless the practitioner (not the patient) objects—you will hardly be surprised to know that this has never happened. And yet for the much more serious issue of striking off the medical register the Disciplinary Committee of the General Medical Council normally sits in public. In view of the kinds of facts found against practitioners who have still been allowed to continue to function under the scheme, one might have thought that their patients would be entitled to know. For example, a dentist who violated the regulations by extracting teeth without prior approval, who also had illegally exacted fees from a patient and failed to keep proper records, was allowed to remain on the National Health Service list. And if I, a newcomer to a district, obtain a dentist's name from the telephone book, should I not be entitled to know, before becoming his paying patient, that he has been removed from the National Health list because water is not laid on in his surgery and there is no spittoon or washbasin? I have been referring of course only to actual cases decided under the post-war health service legislation.

Under pressure from the profession, the Regulations have since the early days been weighted even more in favour of the practitioner. For example, the committee of the local executive council has a lay deputy chairman in case the chairman is absent. Not surprisingly, he was originally allowed under the Act to sit as well as the chairman in order to gain experience, although he was not allowed to vote. The professions objected on the ground that this weighted the tribunal unfairly against them; the Ministry of course then changed the law, so that even his right to join in discussion has been taken away.

Whenever any criticisms of the National Health Service bodies are made the answer is always the same: the practitioners are content with the arrangements, which have always worked to their satisfaction. Detailed proposals for improvement in the system made in 1968 by the Council on Tribunals have not been acted on.

Let me make one final illustration of my point that the procedure and substance should be under continuous scrutiny.

Complaints are made from time to time that doctors will not accept coloured patients under the scheme. Suppose that when such a coloured person protests to the local executive council it does assign him to a doctor, that doctor can still ignore the council's order, safe in the knowledge that the patient still has no legal remedy against the doctor.

CHAPTER 3

THE SUPERVISION OF TRIBUNALS

FRANKS COMMITTEE REPORT

I AM of course not forgetting that a great deal of important supervisory work of administrative tribunals has taken place in the last dozen years or so. In 1955 the Government appointed a committee under the chairmanship of Lord Franks to consider the constitution and working of tribunals. The Committee took much valuable evidence, and in 1957 presented a deservedly and widely acclaimed report. If I devote less attention to it than you expect, that is not because I do not admire the Report. It is because I believe that you have not come here to listen at great length to a paraphrase of a Command Paper published in the 1950s and a summary of the ways in which its proposals have been implemented. However misguided you may be, I have to assume that you want my views on today's problems rather than an account of Lord Franks' findings. Now the most important task is to consider what remains to be done. I must stress that all the comments I have so far made about tribunals are valid as of today, notwithstanding the Franks Report and the reforms introduced in its train.

The Franks Committee stressed that the procedures of tribunals should be open, fair and impartial, and made detailed recommendations to those ends. Much has been done in consequence. Those appearing before tribunals are given adequate notice about the case before it comes up for decision. They are allowed to attend and give evidence at the hearing; sometimes they have been allowed to be represented by a lawyer. On the other hand nothing has been done to implement the Report's recommendations about legal aid before tribunals. Tribunals have still not been given powers to subpoena witnesses to give evidence or to produce documents.

Council on Tribunals

The most important recommendation was that a Council on Tribunals should be set up in order (among other matters) to keep under review the constitution and working of tribunals. A Council on Tribunals was set up with commendable speed under the Tribunals and Inquiries Act 1958, and it now operates under the Tribunals and Inquiries Act 1971. The Franks Committee was particularly concerned that the Council should appoint members of tribunals, other than chairmen who should be appointed by the Lord Chancellor. No such powers have been given to the Council on Tribunals. The Act of 1971 empowers the Lord Chancellor to appoint panels of authorised chairmen of tribunals. Although the Act did not go on to implement the further recommendation in the Franks Report that all chairmen should be lawyers, great improvements have occurred. The Lord Chancellor's department is obviously taking much more care about appointments than was previously taken, and in practice most chairmen being appointed are lawyers.

The Council on Tribunals is a body of part-timers. It runs on a very small salary and expenses budget. Within the limits of its budget and powers it has done as much as could be expected in supervising administrative tribunals. In effect it performs two tasks with regard to existing tribunals. When it receives a complaint about the procedure at a tribunal it investigates and, if necessary, makes representations to the governmental body concerned. Its concern is to discover whether the procedure is unfair, and, if so, to press for a change in future. It has no compulsory powers. In addition a member of the Council will occasionally give notice to a tribunal that he intends to be a spectator at a specific hearing; after attending, he will fill in a printed form reporting on the tribunal to the Council.

This account will make it obvious that there is no effective supervision of the administrative tribunals in this country. Take personnel first. Members simply have not the time to make frequent visits to particular local tribunals. It would be interesting to know how often, if at all, a lawyer-member of the Council has inspected a tribunal in the north west in the last ten years. It would be safe to assume that he has not inspected one hearing in a thousand in the area. I think it fair to say that the Council is playing no effective part in ensuring that the personnel are discharging their duties competently. Unannounced and frequent visits would be necessary. In order to assess the quality of the chairman's paper work random examination of decision files would have to be made. In fact not only does the Council not do this, it has not even the power. I am not criticising the Council; I repeat that it has not the resources to do more than it is doing already. I am emphasising that its supervision of tribunals is so slight as to be ineffective. It is unlikely to discover the existence of incompetent tribunal members.

The Council is authorised to review "the working" of tribunals. "Working" is a vague expression. At the very least it must include all procedural aspects of a tribunal. What I have said about those tribunals which I have examined at length, will surely convince you that very occasional attendance, together with the following up of the odd complaint from a citizen, cannot possibly be enough. There is not a single active set of tribunals which either the Franks Committee or the Council on Tribunals has examined with sufficient thoroughness. And I am still talking only about procedures: that is, the paper work from the starting of the proceedings to their end, and the hearing of the case.

The Council has obviously been in difficulty with the word "working." Very occasionally it has recognised, what I trust my survey has made inescapably clear, that an investigation which confined itself to the procedural elements would be tackling the comparatively unimportant, the simple and straightforward aspects of a tribunal. That is why no doubt the Council has investigated the legal principles which rent tribunals apply in assessing a reasonable rent. If those legal principles are part of the "working" it would seem to follow that all the law which all tribunals within its scope apply must be within the Council's jurisdiction. But that is not the way the Council has operated. Almost all the time it has contented itself with the simple issues of procedure. Again I do not criticise the Council. My main point is how relatively unimportant that aspect of a tribunal's work is. The boundary between procedure and substance is indistinct, but what really matters is whether a tribunal is performing efficiently in its area of activity. Then far and away the most important questions are the kinds of decisions which it is making, and whether it has the appropriate powers and scope. This is not the Council's business, and it is nobody else's. Here there is a most serious gap in our control of administrative tribunals.

I have an intense desire that the Welfare State be successful. I am sure that tribunals are necessary for a flourishing Welfare State. I believe that they can attain a standard of efficiency way ahead of what our ordinary courts have achieved. That has not yet happened. There is no body whose job it is to have a detailed knowledge of what is being done. Every kind of tribunal should have been the subject of exhaustive study. The law which each operates, as well as its constitution and procedures, should be under continuous review by a body, which has the resources and expertise to do it. The new Select Committees of the House of Commons, which the Government has set up in the last few years, do not have the time, the resources or perhaps even the inclination, to do what I want.

Whatever changes are made, I know that administrative tribunals will remain far from perfect. I said before that they are not a Rolls-Royce system. The more cheap family saloons and the fewer Rolls-Royces there are, the greater is the need for good servicing and repair facilities. So it is with tribunals. In the background we must always have the ordinary courts standing by on call when there is a breakdown of a tribunal. A tribunal might exceed its jurisdiction or threaten to do so. It might arrive at an erroneous legal answer, even though it is entitled to reach a decision on the particular point. The solution seems simple; a uniform quick procedure whereby an aggrieved citizen can ask the High Court to decide whether the tribunal was empowered to act and whether even so its decision was correct in law. Simple, yes, but we just don't have it.

The Inadequacies of Judicial Review

Who is to blame for that? The courts themselves, chiefly. They have failed to work out a simple scheme of review. Instead they have cluttered us up with an incoherent, complex, inefficient and jumbled mass of rules. There are a number of different remedies from which the citizen must choose: certiorari, mandamus, prohibition, injunction and declaration, case stated, and appeal on point of law. Sometimes Parliament has given another remedy in a specific case. The courts have elaborated for us—and we are not grateful—a series of rules which define, or more often fail to define, the scope of each of these remedies. Each of them has its hidden pitfalls. If the citizen's lawyer chooses the wrong one, even though his case is good, the citizen's claim will be dismissed. He will be told to start all over again at his own expense, and also at the cost of meeting all the legal expenses incurred by his opponent in making a good defence which had no substantive merits. If the tribunal is part of central government, you can never seek an injunction; for injunctions do not lie against the Crown. If the function is administrative and not judicial, certiorari is unavailable. If the tribunal acts within its jurisdiction but has gone wrong in law, mandamus is no use, but certiorari may be. It then depends whether you can see the error by reading the document which embodies the decision—the error must be on the face of the record. As every tribunal chairman knows, then, if you want to evade judicial scrutiny, don't put in writing any more than you can help. Maybe the citizen later persuades the tribunal to volunteer its reasons for deciding against him—he will now find a new obstacle. He has only six months in which to challenge by certiorari or mandamus. If only he had asked for a declaration. But does a declaration lie for errors of law within the jurisdiction? The judges cannot make up their minds about this. And so we go on.

All of this is so intolerable that it is miraculous that it has been allowed to survive. The Franks Committee were told all about this mess by the greatest expert in the country and were guided by him on what to do about it. They ignored the advice and expressed themselves as largely satisfied with things as they were. They merely expressed the opinion that there should be an appeal on points of law, but they did not think that it was right for them even to recommend what form this additional remedy should take. What they were sure of was that the other remedies were not unduly complex and should be left alone, except that the period of six months within which to challenge by certiorari should be shortened.

I say dogmatically that the Franks Committee was wrong in successfully recommending the perpetuation of these complexities. Its Canute-like posture should not avail. The experts in the field all agree that these involved rules have no merit and should be swept away. The courts will not do it; Parliament should, and quickly. The solution is beautifully easy, as countries like South Africa have long since discovered, and as the Law Commission has also recently found. All we need is one single procedure for applications to the Divisional Court of the Queen's Bench Division. It does not matter whether the citizen is aggrieved because the tribunal had no jurisdiction to act, or it refused to act when it ought to have acted, or reached a decision wrong in law, or whether the error was on the record, or whether it failed to give him a fair and appropriate hearing. All we need is just one form of application to cover all these cases.

The Franks Committee did make one sensible and necessary recommendation connected with the present matter, which unfortunately Parliament has neglected to implement properly. I have shown how social security tribunals record the evidence, their findings and their reasons. You will say " But, of course. How else would anybody dream of dispensing justice? " Well, at the time of the Franks Report very few tribunals indeed carried out their functions in this manner, which elementary standards of fairness seem to demand. My recent investigations show that little change has occurred since that time. The fault is Parliament's, for its response to the Franks Committee recommendation was half-hearted. By the Tribunals and Inquiries Act 1971 certain tribunals are required " to furnish a statement, either written or oral, of the reasons for the decision if requested, on or before the giving or notification of the decision, to state the reasons." You will notice there is never a duty under this Act to make findings of fact, still less to summarise evidence. There is no duty at all unless requested, and that duty is only to give reasons. And unless the request is made when the decision is given, it may be too late.

Take the ordinary case before an administrative tribunal. The citizen is never told in his papers notifying him of the hearing of his right to ask for reasons. Neither the clerk nor the chairman tells him at the hearing. When he loses and is fobbed off by the tribunal without explanation, he then goes to a solicitor for the first time. The solicitor asks the tribunal for its reasons, to be told " Too late—if you don't ask for them at the time, you are not entitled to them." A former member of the Council on Tribunals wrote in his book that " most tribunals give their reasons as a matter of course." In the context he was obviously talking only about tribunals which had no special statutory duty to do so, that is, he was not referring to social security tribunals. My experience of tribunals generally was so contrary to his that, within the next month after reading it, I made a point of visiting several different tribunals. Not one of them gave reasons within the meaning of the Act when announcing its decision. Of course I dare say they would if a member of the Council had given a fortnight's notice of his intention to attend! I have mentioned before the obvious reason why chairmen don't volunteer reasons—they don't want to be caught out. But there are other consequences. My talks with the Press who regularly cover tribunals show that the chairmen who never give reasons are well known to journalists. Their other common ploy is not to let the Press know about hearings—it ought to be compulsory for all notices of all tribunal hearings to be posted in one place in every town—as the Press are at the mercy of those in charge of each tribunal. These chairmen effectively ensure that the Franks recommendations about access for the Press are frustrated—the Press simply will not attend hearings (even if they know of them) if no reasons are given, so that the public is denied that opportunity which it would otherwise have of knowing what was going on. The chairmen avoid the risk that the Press might criticise their decisions, and that such Press comment might come to the attention of their supervising Ministry or of the Lord Chancellor's department.

I have talked at length about these matters directly within my own experience in order to further the right of the citizen to justice in the Welfare State. Our tribunals are a splendid innovation. We must be diligent to see that they function as efficiently and justly as possible. At present they are better than they have ever been. I have tried to indicate what remains to be done so that we could say that our system of administrative tribunals is as fair and efficient as any in the world.

CHAPTER 4

LICENSING

ONE of the cardinal features of the Welfare State is the way in which our activities are interfered with or controlled by government in the public interest. There is a great deal of this in time of war or other emergency, but now it is also an accepted phenomenon in normal times. Its legal elements have not received much attention. I remember some 25 years ago realising how little was known or written about our systems of controls. I then spent years examining some of them, especially the emergency ones connected with rationing and control of scarce commodities. Just as I was bringing that part of the research to a close, most of those controls were swept away. Rather impetuously, perhaps, I then abandoned the whole project. I am not aware that any other systematic examination of the subject has since been made, and yet it remains of great importance. In particular, I want to take a close look at our licensing systems. And by licensing I do not mean liquor licensing. It is true that that was our earliest form of licensing—in 1552 it started—but today it is no more important than many other forms. Every year more and more schemes of licensing and regulation are introduced or mooted.

REASONS FOR THE GROWTH OF LICENSING

There are some perfectly sound reasons for the widespread resort to licensing. Experience shows that far too many activities cause avoidable harm to innocent victims. Of course the law of crime will be available to deal with any criminal offences committed in the course of those activities and, if harm is caused by wrongful conduct, the law will require the wrongdoer to pay damages to the victim. But why stand by and wait for the harm to occur? It is much better to prevent the damage from being done at all. Take the most obvious example of all: driving a car. If a motorist drives dangerously, no doubt he can be fined, or even imprisoned, under the criminal law. If he disables a pedestrian through his careless driving, of course that pedestrian can sue in the courts for damages. But that is not enough; we want to keep down the number of road accidents. And so we license drivers; we won't let them drive without a licence, and we require them to pass a test before they can have the licence. We believe that we will reduce the number of accidents if drivers have to prove their competence before they drive alone—we are not content to leave it to the law to punish and redress grievances after harm has been done. All this seems obvious, yet there had been motoring for over 30 years before we introduced licensing by tests and Northern Ireland did so only recently. It is mainly to prevent harm from occurring in foreseeable ways that we have accepted control by licensing. I give you a few examples.

Very often the main consideration is physical safety. Before you can store explosives or petrol, therefore, you need a licence. Licences are required for passenger-carrying aircraft and for seaside pleasure boats. One of the reasons why theatres are licensed is to control the fire hazard. A more recent example is the requirement that sites for nuclear power stations have to be licensed.

Licences are often required in order to minimise the chance that crimes of dishonesty will be committed. You may not deal in stocks and shares without a licence; if you are operating a unit trust, a licence is needed. House-to-house collections are forbidden unless permission has been granted beforehand.

Other activities endanger health. That is why a licence is required in order to run a dairy. For the same reason ice-cream manufacturers have to be licensed.

The law is always especially solicitous for the welfare of the young and infirm. No doubt, those who poison inmates of old people's homes, having previously induced them to make a will in their favour, will be dealt with by the criminal law. Parliament takes the view that it is better to make proprietors of such homes obtain a licence before they set up in business. Accordingly, nursing homes, homes for the disabled, children's nurseries and children's homes also have to be licensed. Children under the age of 16 may not take part in certain kinds of public performance without the permission of the local authority. Theatrical employers are licensed. Characteristically, we extend this type of protection to animals. If you want to train performing animals, you will first have to get a licence. Horse-slaughterers and operators of knackers' yards are similarly controlled, and so are riding stables.

We have a crime of public nuisance which covers a miscellany of interferences with public rights, including rights on highways. In order to cut down these nuisances many activities require licensing. Street collections for charity, hawkers and pedlars, and sometimes processions, are examples; car rallies are a recent addition. This is also the best justification for the need to have music, singing and dancing licences in places of public entertainment.

The detection of crime is buttressed by licensing provisions. Manufacturers and holders of firearms are regulated in this way. Pawnbrokers, metal dealers and marine store dealers have to be licensed. No doubt for the same reason game dealers have been licensed since 1831.

One of the great problems of the twentieth-century State has been how to acknowledge and safeguard the public element in those organisations which provide essential services. In many cases, such as coal, electricity and gas, the technically simple expedient of nationalisation has been resorted to. Greater legal problems result, if nationalisation is rejected, but public control is nonetheless seen to be necessary. Perhaps the most important and complex illustration is passenger and goods transport. Licensing authorities handle applications to set up passenger services; the fitness of the applicant, the need for a service, and the availability of alternative transport are all considered. Control is exercised over the safety of the vehicles and the competence of drivers and conductors. There is similar detailed control over the carrying of goods by road transport. Another example under this head is the licence to operate a television station. No organisation may do so, except with the permission of the Minister of Posts and Telecommunications, who permits the B.B.C. to televise, or the Independent Broadcasting Authority, which is responsible for allotting commercial television franchises.

The law has always given remedies to those who suffer from the incompetence of persons practising a public calling. The inadequacy of this protection for the public has long been evident: it is not enough to give the victim a claim for damage suffered. Consequently, entry to many professional bodies, the law, medicine and dentristry, for example, is controlled by Act of Parliament. The right to practise must be given by an authorised body, before a person may hold himself out as entitled to practise in those professions.

Especially in time of war and other emergency, we find it necessary to restrict the distribution of scarce commodities. Many will recall the vast battery of controls which we had from 1939 to 1951; food was severely rationed, and caterers had to have licences both to trade and to obtain commodities. A large separate branch of the Board of Trade handled import and export licensing. Scarce materials were controlled: for example, a licence was required to repair buildings or ships. Some of these licences persist today. Best known is the licence needed to travel abroad with foreign currency beyond a certain limit.

All of what I have been describing so far about licensing is so sensible that you may be asking: "What can there be to comment on?" I can best answer that by embarking on a more detailed examination.

Disadvantages of Licensing

I will consider first whether there are always good reasons for licensing particular activities. I have mentioned that a licence is often required before a person may practise a certain profession. This system is open to abuse. A particular occupation obviously gains in prestige when entry is regulated by statute. But if the right to admit is entrusted by Parliament to members of the occupation themselves, great dangers ensue. If it is made an offence to carry on that occupation without a licence, the existing members can keep down numbers and put up their charges to the public in consequence.

This has become a great evil in the United States. Grave diggers, egg graders, yacht salesmen, tile layers and hundreds of other similar trades have obtained statutory protection from some states. Every year hundreds of fresh occupations seek to get on the band-wagon.

There are signs in the United Kingdom too that particular trades have seen the advantages in licensing and have pressed for this legislative cushioning. The trend needs to be carefully watched. The only relevant question should be whether it is for the public benefit. Of course licensing will be for the advantage of those already in the profession or trade. If it means that competent persons are prevented from competing and that the public has to pay more for services, it is wholly objectionable. Even with the professions which have been licensed for a long time, there is room for argument about the merits of the system. Take the legal profession. Of course nobody should be allowed to call himself a solicitor unless he has satisfied the requirements of the Solicitors Act. The law does not give solicitors a monopoly in the field of advice on the law; if you choose to go to a tax consultant for advice on a point of income tax law, he is entitled to charge you, although he has no professional qualifications. And yet a person may not charge for drawing up a conveyance of a house unless he is a solicitor. You may go to a firm of solicitors where no qualified solicitor handles the conveyancing matter at any stage, where the whole of the work is done by an unadmitted clerk and yet you are charged the same as if a professionally qualified person had handled the matter. Some may not think it immediately obvious why that is lawful, even though the client is not told that his adviser is unqualified, whereas a member of the public, with his eyes open, who voluntarily prefers to pay less to have a conveyance drawn for him at a smaller fee by a man who openly states that he is not a solicitor, is participating in an illegal transaction.

Liquor licensing illustrates how there may be good reason for licensing, and yet a system may be abused by those making money out of the consequent scarcity value. No doubt, when this licensing was first introduced, it was thought to have merit as a means of curbing drunkenness. But why should free enterprise not operate? Why should the supermarket not be free to sell wine and spirits for consumption off the premises? Under the present system, areas of slum clearance retain unnecessary public houses, because brewers will not give up a valuable franchise, whereas other new areas have far fewer facilities in relation to the population, because licences are hard to come by and issue of new ones is strongly opposed by those who have them already. It is arguable that whatever protection of morals is attained by liquor licensing this is more than offset by the expense and social inconvenience which it causes.

There are other areas where the main consequence of licensing seems to be to confer an unearned tax-free asset on the licensee. Typical was the scandal in the 1960s about apples. Under pressure from the National Farmers' Union, British apple growers have been protected, since the early 1950s, from foreign competition because imports of apples have been subject to licensing controls. Some licensees would sell their licences to others and perhaps earn in consequence £30,000 a year without importing a single apple; they had obtained from the Board of Trade the all-important and uniquely valuable import licence. A governmental committee has revealed the same abuse in transport licensing. New hauliers could not get established in the industry without paying huge premiums to the holders of existing licences.

The licensing system also exposes itself to contempt and ridicule in that so many out-dated and now irrelevant provisions remain on the statute book. To read these provisions is a fascinating study of Britain's economic and social history. For example, and this was part of Liverpool's history, you cannot be a passage broker or an emigrant broker without a licence. A throwback of course to the times when Cunard was not the only shipping company taking passengers down the Mersey to pioneer in the United States. And if your urge for free enterprise makes you want to set up a massage establishment you will be frustrated until you get a licence authorising you to do so. You need a licence to be a gangmaster of farm labourers—very necessary no doubt—but I should have thought it much more important to control building gangs whose avoidance of the laws relating to tax and social security is notorious—those on the lump need no licence. It sometimes seems that whenever a case hits the front page of the Press for a day or two, especially if it is about the time when Members of Parliament are balloting for power to promote a private Bill, a new licensing device will be born. This happened, for example, with the Hypnotism Act 1952. A nineteen-year-old girl volunteered to be hypnotised during a music-hall performance by a stage hypnotist. The girl was ill for months afterwards, until a medically trained hypnotist removed the hypnotic effects. She successfully claimed damages in an action against the music-hall hypnotist. The publicity induced an M.P. who was successful in the Private Members' ballot to introduce a Bill to license stage hypnotists. The Bill was passed, so that the licensing powers for musical entertainments were extended to hypnotism.

I have said that licensing is often introduced to reinforce criminal law and the law relating to compensation. But first one ought to be sure that the existing law is inadequate. Take theatre censorship. For over 200 years Parliament had provided that plays could not be put on in public, unless the licence of the Lord Chamberlain had been obtained beforehand. Perhaps we could agree that plays ought not to preach treasonable doctrines, or to shower the audience with filthy obscenities, or to make unjustified attacks on the reputation of living people. Yet have we needed censorship to take care of those? After all, we have the law of treason, of obscenity and of libel and slander. What used to happen with regard to theatre censorship illustrates the risk I am at present discussing. A play would be refused a licence even though it did not contravene the existing criminal law or the law of libel. No play was allowed about any member of the Royal Family (even though he died 60 years ago); or about dead historical figures whose relatives were still alive. Religious plays were severely restricted. In short, without any specific authority from Parliament, this form of licensing took control far beyond anything which the law had previously encompassed. If the law needed to protect every member of the Royal Family alive in this century, and every dead historical figure with a surviving relative, was it not for Parliament, rather than the Lord Chamberlain, to say so? No doubt that was why the Theatres Act 1968 abolished theatre censorship.

Taxi licensing is an excellent example of how a system of licensing, for which there is justification, can incur merited criticism for its inability to keep up with the times. I agree that the public should be guarded against the risk of dangerous vehicles, of exorbitant fares and of drivers of bad character or those who are ignorant of routes. But why is this protection necessary only if the taxi plies for hire? Why are the mini-cabs, the telephone-hire cabs, immune from all these dangers so long as they operate outside London? Is it in the public interest to restrict the number of taxis, to declare in many cities that ordinary standard saloon models are unsafe, to make the public seek a taxi only at authorised stands, and to allow taxi owners to sell the valuable scarce licences for four figure sums in seaside towns and inland spas where they are such a valuable franchise?

A great deal of licensing has been introduced for administrative convenience. It is much easier for the police to charge somebody with operating without a licence than it is to prove that they have committed whatever offence it is that is supposed to make licensing desirable. We should be on our guard against sanctioning interferences with liberty which have no more solid justification than that. If it is merely a question of keeping track of persons engaged in a particular activity, a requirement that a person registers himself would be enough—it would not be necessary that he also obtains permission to engage in the operation.

I believe that a great deal of licensing is for the benefit of the citizen. Yet we are all rightly suspicious of all encroachments on our liberty. We must be very careful not to allow interferences for no good reason. We do not want to be regulated unless it makes us better off. There is another danger from ill-considered licensing. The opportunity of many people to profiteer at the expense of others is curbed by licensing. They are powerful men who will strive hard to regain their freedom to exploit the unwary. They must not be given a pretext for the restoration of their old ways—they must not be able to point to unnecessary or unreasonable licensing systems.

Who Grants Licences?

I consider next who decides whether a licence shall be granted. The power is scattered willy-nilly among a large number of different bodies. It may surprise you to know how many powers of this kind the police have. The list varies from town to town. Here are some of the licences controlled by the police. Firearms, street collections, processions, marine store dealers, pedlars, ferrymen, pleasure boats, theatres, car rallies, car park attendants, shoeblacks, taxis and their drivers, domestic service agencies, employment agencies and theatrical employers. Sometimes, as in the case of licences of pedlars, the chief constable can delegate the final decision to any officer; some statutes, for example, the House to House Collections Act 1939, restrict it to inspectors or those of higher rank. Do we really want the final say in decisions which will take away a man's livelihood to rest with policemen? And have they the time to spare from detecting criminals?

Large numbers of licensing powers are distributed among local authorities, sometimes all local authorities, on other occasions only the top tier authorities. House to house collections, nursing homes, taxis, petroleum, explosives, cinemas, theatres, betting tracks, training performing animals, pet shops and animal boarding kennels are random examples. I will discuss later the crucial question of whether applicants for these licences get a fair hearing.

Many licensing functions are entrusted to justices of the peace. Almost always this is a relic from the times when they were the only local administrative body. They are in charge of liquor licensing and they also have to license billiard halls. They share other licensing functions with local authorities, for example, the licensing of theatres and cinemas. This produces the following anomaly. It sometimes happens that the licensing Act does not mention any right of appeal. In that case, where it is the justices who have the licensing power, there is an implied right of appeal to the court of quarter sessions, but, if the local authority is the licensing body, there is no appeal from its decision.

Sometimes special tribunals are set up. The most important example is in the field of transport licensing. The country is divided into ten areas, to each of which three officers are appointed. The chairman of these three is authorised to grant carriers' licences, and an appeal lies to the Road Haulage Division of a national tribunal, the Transport Tribunal. He also grants heavy goods vehicle drivers' licences, with an appeal to a magistrates' court. The three officers grant licences to run passenger services and licences for the vehicles and the operators. Appeals lie to the Secretary of State for the Environment, who appoints an inspector to hold an inquiry. Another example of a special tribunal is that in charge of appeals on licensing voluntary children's homes. Sometimes a commission is set up to supervise an industry: for instance, the Herring Industry Board is empowered to license herring boats.

Many licensing functions are centred in Ministries. Economic controls are located there, so that these government departments were the most important licensing bodies of all during the war. The relevant Acts merely say that the Minister licenses, but in practice his staff do it. The details of these arrangements within Ministries had never been revealed until post-war scandals forced the setting up of the Committee on Intermediaries under the chairmanship of Sir Edwin Herbert (later Lord Tangley)—the Committee reported in 1950 and set out in great detail the arrangements within every Ministry. Ministers have a miscellaneous set of licensing functions other than economic controls, for example, they grant licences to practise vivisection, to sell wild birds and to run an abortion clinic. Sometimes, and often unpredictably, the Minister is the tribunal of appeal, although in practice he then will no doubt appoint another to investigate for him. For example, an appeal against the refusal of a licence to carry out a house-to-house collection lies to the Home Secretary. Sometimes he is required to take advice before deciding the appeal, but he can still decide as he wishes. There has been a recent tendency to set up bodies which are required to consider applications for licences and to advise the Minister whether he shall grant a licence, which it remains in his sole discretion to do. The Medicines Act 1968 follows this pattern on drug control.

When a profession is licensed it always succeeds in persuading Parliament to let it run its own affairs—no public participation is sanctioned. This is true even of the Medical Practices Committee which decides, subject to appeal to the Secretary of State for the Social Services, which doctor-applicants shall be allowed to run National Health Service practices in a defined area. The Independent Broadcasting Authority decides which television companies shall be allowed in commercial television.

SOURCES OF LICENSING POWER

One would have thought that it would be a simple matter to find out what licensing powers exist. Nothing of the kind. Most of the powers are contained in Acts of Parliament, but many of these Acts are adoptive: that is to say that each local authority can please itself whether it will extend the Act to its area. An even more confusing variant is provided by taxi licensing, which is compulsory in some areas but optional in others. Sometimes one finds that the Act sets up a licensing scheme, but a Minister has subsequently exercised his power of suspending the operation of the licensing provisions in that Act.

Local Acts are of great importance. Manchester has local Acts for licensing massage establishments, food vendors, hairdressers, servants' registries, theatrical agencies, brokers and market porters, among others. A recent Birmingham Act prevents houses from being let in multi-occupation unless a licence has been given. If the council thinks that it would detract from the amenities of the area, or that the applicant is unsuitable, it may refuse permission. The practical effect of this power has been that Birmingham has been able for the most part to confine its coloured citizens to particular areas. This satisfies citizens who do not wish their neighbourhoods to be "contaminated," but it obviously creates the risk of establishing ghettoes. Hertfordshire's local Acts also cover boxing and wrestling, music and dancing, and employment agencies.

So widespread is licensing by local Act that in the 1930s Captain Bourne M.P., who specialised in this topic, produced, under House of Commons authority, standard clauses for licensing provisions in local Acts, which laid particular stress on ensuring a fair hearing. The plan was that local authorities who were promoting private Bills could incorporate such clauses *in toto* if they desired, knowing that their form would meet with parliamentary approval.

It is difficult enough for the citizen to know the contents of local Acts. The situation is more confused because many of the conditions to be attached to licences, and the procedures regulating their grant, are found, not in the Act, but in local by-laws. The judges have several times strongly citicised this practice on the ground that it is unfair to the citizen who cannot be expected to track down the details of by-laws, but it still persists.

Registration

I have suggested that there is often merit in registration, as distinct from licensing. It may be an unfair restraint on a citizen's liberty to require him to obtain permission before he carries out an activity, but it may be reasonable that there should be an official and accessible list of persons engaged in that activity. Parliament has recognised this by providing for registration of many occupations. Unfortunately and inexcusably, many an Act speaks of registration and not of licensing, and yet when one reads the Act, what poses as registration is in fact licensing. That is to say, the registering body has to satisfy itself about the suitability of the applicant before registering him. For example, cooked meats manufacturers have to be registered; yet the local authority may refuse registration if it believes the place of manufacture to be unhygienic. Conversely, a licence is required before a young child can take part in certain public entertainments, but a local authority is bound to grant the licence if certain conditions are fulfilled.

Procedures

I turn next to the procedures. It would seem obvious that if a person is seeking a licence he is entitled to be heard before a decision unfavourable to him is reached—it may be either a flat rejection, or the imposition of conditions which he regards as onerous. The Bourne Committee on Standard Clauses in Private Bills recognised this, and private Bills which did not specifically give rights to be heard have been rejected by Parliament from time to time. Yet when licensing powers are not conferred on special tribunals, a right to be heard in person is very rarely given. It is the standard practice to deny any hearing for the vast array of licensing functions which have been conferred on Ministers over the years. Even when the Minister is the appellate body, a hearing is not usually given by the Act.

The allocation of television stations—what Lord Thomson of Fleet has called a licence to print money—is a good illustration of this offhand attitude to hearings. In the United States the Federal Communications Commission is required to hold hearings in public on applications for licences. Cross examination of witnesses by counsel is allowed, and reasoned decisions are given. Here, the Independent Broadcasting Authority holds private discussions with such applicants as it chooses to hear and in due course announces who is to be given the licences. Which method is better?

Very few statutes expressly require local authorities to give a hearing. The exceptions are where trade pressure has forced Parliament to do so. For example, sausage manufacturers are controlled by the Food and Drugs Act 1955. Before they can be refused permission to manufacture, the Act says that they are to be given 21 days' notice of the local authorities' intention not to grant permission, and it expressly authorises them to attend a hearing and to be represented by counsel, solicitors or others.

What happens when a right to a hearing before local authorities is not expressly given? My inquiries show that local authorities commonly reach decisions on these licences without affording applicants and objectors the right to be heard. Some local authorities will sometimes allow representations to be made to one of their committees, but nowhere else, although that committee has power merely to recommend to the council. It may be that these local councils are acting illegally in not giving a hearing. I say " it may be " because the decisions of the courts are so confusing and contradictory that nobody knows whether local authorities must hear licensees when the Act is silent on the matter.

Local authorities assert with some justification that they are not equipped to give a hearing in the way that a tribunal does. Take one case in the 1950s. A person aggrieved by a proposed decision of his local authority insisted on a hearing before the council acted on a recommendation against him made by one of its sub-committees. A full meeting of the council was called specially, and the citizen was represented by a barrister. His barrister objected to members of the council sitting, who were members of the sub-committee. The town clerk ignored that challenge and proceeded with the meeting. The citizen appealed to the High Court against the town clerk's ruling. Mr. Justice Gerrard granted an injunction against the council and described the council's attitude as monstrous. The council appealed to the Court of Appeal, but the case was settled out of court. Of course one can sympathise with the dilemma of town clerks in the present state of uncertainty of the law. They do not know whether they are to exclude members of committees from meetings of the council which approve recommendations by those committees about licences; they do not know when they are bound to give a hearing to applicants; they do not know whether a hearing before a committee or sub-committee of the council is enough, or whether a hearing before the full council must be allowed.

One can say with confidence that a vast number of local authority licensing decisions is made in breach of those rules of natural justice which govern hearings by courts and tribunals. Departmental committees on particular aspects of licensing, taxis, for example, have complained about failure to give a hearing before a licence is taken away, but the practice continues. Whatever area of local authority licensing one investigates, one finds that practices vary from authority to authority. Some will entrust investigation to officials, others to policemen, some will even take evidence from police and other persons behind the back of the licensee and decide without giving him the chance to confront these witnesses.

No attempt has ever been made systematically to survey the licensing of local authorities, the variations in content of public Acts, local Acts and by-laws and standing orders. I believe that the results of such a comprehensive investigation would be staggering. It is true that there is often an appeal to the magistrates' courts from the refusal of a licence by a local authority. This power of appeal may be illusory. Frequently a local authority is entitled to attach conditions to the grant or even renewal of a licence. Suppose that a local authority will not renew a licence of an all-night café unless the proprietor agrees to close between 11 p.m. and 5 a.m. What use is his right of appeal to the magistrates' court when the order of the local authority to close down comes into operation before his appeal can be heard? But there are cases where there is no appeal at which there is a right to be heard, even though a man's livelihood is involved—rag flock manufacturing is one example chosen at random. Moreover I do not share the commonly held view that as long as there is an appeal it does not matter whether the original decision is arrived at fairly: the citizen should have confidence in the fairness of proceedings from the start.

I believe that Parliament has shirked its responsibilities in this area. On every aspect of licensing it should have decided whether there was a right to be heard orally or at least to make representations, and whether cross-examination of all evidence was to be permitted. Licensing functions should never have been entrusted to local authorities without clearing up these points, and without also clarifying the respective roles of the local authority and its committees. For myself I doubt whether local authorities are ever satisfactory bodies to conduct hearings in the way tribunals do. If a decision affects a person's livelihood or other rights of his to the extent that hearings and examination of witnesses become necessary, I think that those licensing functions should be taken away from local authorities. The present concern about corruption in local government only emphasises the urgency.

I have talked about licensing by local authorities. Local authorities also make decisions on allocating scarce resources to citizens which, although not called licensing, similarly affect citizens. I refer to the allocation of municipal housing. At the moment, a local authority is free to make any rules it likes for allocation of houses. It need not publish its rules, and many do keep them secret. An applicant is not entitled to be heard; many local authorities conduct their meetings on allocating houses in private; they act on information about applicants, the accuracy of which the applicant cannot dispute because he never sees it. Whether the law should allow decisions of such importance to be made in this manner is surely arguable. Do these procedures meet the requirement that justice must not only be done, it must been seen to be done?

Judicial Review

When I talked about tribunals I attached importance to the review of administrative decisions by the courts. I have just been talking about one serious limitation on that—that the courts often do not insist on a licensing body giving a fair hearing. Very few licensing bodies are required to give reasons for their decisions. This greatly restricts the power of the courts to interfere with their decisions on substantive grounds

—that is why the courts are seldom called upon to review licensing decisions on issues of law or on the grounds that discretion was exercised improperly.

Systems of Inspection

I save to the last my most serious criticism of licensing. Licensing is ordinarily part of a scheme to control some activity. It normally runs in harness with a system of inspection. The big questions about all these arrangements are: How efficient are they? Do they achieve the purposes for which they were ostensibly set up? There is obviously no point in responding to public agitation on a matter by enacting some statutory provisions which look impressive merely on paper. They must be followed up if need be by detailed workable regulations. There must be the staff to carry out inspection; infringements must be detected and punished. When I was first looking at licensing 25 years ago I was struck by its overall inefficiency, and it is still so today.

Take the Falmouth boating disaster in 1966 when 31 lives were lost in a motor boat. At the routine Board of Trade inquiry into the accident the Commissioner seemed surprised that there was nothing to stop unqualified persons taking motor cruisers to sea with a full load of passengers, that the Act did not compel boat proprietors to take out licences, that violations of the Act only resulted in a maximum fine of £5 and that those local authorities which had licensing functions took no steps to prevent unlicensed boats from putting to sea. Of course he advocated an efficient nation-wide system of licensing of pleasure boats—we still have no such system. In line with this was the 1972 fatal Hovercraft accident in the Solent where once again regulations had been disregarded. I contrast that with a holiday I took some years ago in a New

England coastal resort where pleasure boats were required, as a condition of the granting of a licence, to be in radio telephone contact with the nearest coastguard station. There would have been no disaster if this American law had applied to Falmouth.

With distressing regularity, when there is an inquiry into a serious accident supposed to be controlled by licensing, inefficiency is revealed. I recall a petrol explosion in a Bristol garage some years ago, in which 11 persons were killed. The garage proprietor did not hold the requisite licence to store petrol, the Watch Committee appeared not to have supervised the numbers or nature of new licensees and had left it to the police force, where three technically unqualified officers were put in charge. Or take the failure in 1967 of the Board of Trade to prevent Davies Investments from continuing to advertise for deposits from the public when its accounts revealed huge doubtful debts—it was left to *The Guardian* newspaper to protect the public.

Another example of ineffective supervision used to be that provided by betting, gaming and lotteries legislation. The Acts of the 1960s had failed to prevent international widespread criminal exploitation of its provisions. In 1968, therefore, the Government was driven to introduce for the first time efficient controls. Licensing committees now license clubs where commercial gaming takes place, and objectors are entitled to be heard. A new gaming inspectorate has access to all licensed clubs for the purpose of ensuring that the law, and the conditions inserted in licences, are being complied with. The Home Secretary and the Gaming Board have drawn up detailed regulations. Nobody is allowed to work in a gaming club without a licence from that Board. Suppliers of gaming machines are also controlled by the Board.

That last example and my next demonstrate how much more difficult it is to have efficient control when Parliament decides to have the activity conducted by private enterprise. I refer now to the testing of cars which is done by licensed garage testers. It has of course become a national scandal that garages were freely licensing unroadworthy vehicles. And why? Simply because both the licensing and inspection provisions have been inefficient. Spot checks of lorries made by inspectors show that very few of them also conform to the law's safety requirements.

Recent legislation in areas such as drug control suggests that Governments are now realising the interlocking nature of these controls, with licensing by expert bodies, carefully drawn regulations and efficient inspection arrangements. The thalidomide tragedy could not have occurred in the 1970s. Of course, as always, balance is important. Controls must not become so complex and watertight that injustice results; some would make that criticism of gaming controls now.

Some Needed Reforms

Welcome though these new developments are, they do not put right widespread present defects. It is nobody's business to supervise our present licensing arrangements. The vast majority of these licensing agencies are outside the purview of the Council on Tribunals. The Parliamentary Commissioner, about whom I shall be talking later, has no jurisdiction over many of them. It is only when lives are lost unnecessarily in some accident, so that a public outcry follows, that a leisurely examination of licensing defects in a particular area is made. The present system has great defects. It is vastly complex, much of it is unnecessary and outdated, there is a great deal of unfairness in its operation and it fails to achieve the worthwhile objects for which it was set up. If we are to have controls, it is our business to see that they work properly. I hope that I have shown how they fail to do so.

It is the more necessary that we put this part of our house in order when we notice how frequently more and more licensing controls are advocated. I do not of course subscribe to the view that controls are a good thing in themselves. What I do say is that when a case is made out they must be fair and efficient. I am the keener to maintain these standards because, whatever political party is in office, it appears to regard further extension of regulation as inevitable. The need is the greater now that membership of the European Economic Community has imposed new licensing functions on us; for example, the licensing of seed producers and merchants. I do not doubt that every year will see new licensing statutes; for example the Employment Agencies Act 1973 and the Dumping at Sea Act 1974.

Efficient licensing systems might also be used for a further purpose. The Costs in Criminal Cases Act 1973 now enables the victims of crime, on an order of the criminal court, to be compensated by the criminals for their losses. It could be salutary if licence-evading criminals also could be ordered on conviction to pay damages to their victims.

In many spheres, we have what I regard as a regrettable tendency to allow organisations whose activities closely bear on public rights to control themselves—it is essentially the same as the gild system of the Middle Ages.

Although I am especially concerned with licensing now, I should say in passing that that practice is widespread elsewhere. I deplore the fact that the Police Act 1964 allows complaints by citizens against the police to be considered only by policemen, and I cannot accept the argument that complaints against policemen are matters only of discipline within the force; I believe that they are equally questions of human rights. Or take a very different example. I don't see why the party whips should decide in private conclave with the B.B.C. how many party political broadcasts shall be inflicted on us, and how many there shall be by each party. Or take the signal failure of the Stock Exchange Council, despite Government prodding, to protect shareholders against take-over tactics by market operators and companies which prejudicially affect the shareholders.

I must concentrate on the licensing aspect, and look first at advertising. The United States has a Federal Trades Commission, which, among other matters, controls the content of advertising; it is able to prevent the continued publication of false advertising by making orders, enforceable in the courts, that advertising which it finds to be misleading shall cease. We leave it to a voluntary body within the advertising industry to protect the customer against false advertising: there is no supervision of advertising by court or tribunal.

An incident at Christmas 1967 is revealing. Thousands of the public were defrauded through sending money to a wine merchant in response to his advertisement in the Press offering liquor at cut prices. The liquor was not supplied; no doubt the gullible public thought that the advertisement was genuine because it appeared in the respectable national newspapers. Liquor retailers then pressed the Home Office to tighten up on liquor licensing in order to protect them against unfair competition. One might have been forgiven for thinking that the vital issue was whether the law should start to control fraudulent advertising. Of course the advertising industry's own machinery had proved useless as a protection for the public in this instance. Presumably they had not checked the commercial fidelity of the advertiser, despite the well-founded suspicion of other liquor retailers.

With the vast increases in holidays abroad, travel agencies are doing a large amount of business. Every year disappointed holiday makers lose their deposits with fraudulent agencies or fail to receive what they were led to expect. Pressure groups like the Association of British Travel Agents have successfully persuaded successive governments to leave it to them to wield voluntary controls. These voluntary controls have failed. The fair trading inspectorates of local authorities have striven mightily to utilise the Trade Descriptions Act 1968 so as to curb the more blatant lies of the industry. Yet licensing and guarantee and deposit of assets under statutory control seem inevitable if the public is to be protected. Did the voluntary system fully protect clients of Court Line in 1974?

Another topical illustration is road traffic insurance. Insurance companies are largely free to impose whatever premiums and conditions they like in automobile policies. If the motorist has failed to comply with one of the conditions in the fine print the insurance company is entitled to reject his claim, even though his failure is totally unrelated to his claim. Until recently motor insurance companies have also been virtually free from financial supervision, with the result that thousands of motorists have in the last few years been defrauded by their insurance companies. It could not have happened in the United States, nor could motorists there have onerous conditions imposed on them at the will of the insurers. There insurance commissioners set up by statute control the contents of policies, the premium rates and the financial stability of companies. It is interesting too that the more extensive licensing of the United States often enables them to achieve legislative ends which are less easy to attain here.

Take legislation against racial discrimination with regard to housing. In the United States estate agents are licensed. Consider how much easier it becomes to keep down housing discrimination when your estate agent is liable to have his licence to trade revoked on proof that he unlawfully discriminated in negotiating a sale or lease of a house or flat.

The system of licensing controls which I have described in this lecture is an important attempt to do justice in the Welfare State. Although I do not favour regulation unless a strong case is made out for it, I accept that great benefits have been conferred on Englishmen by provisions of this kind. If I am critical of some aspects it is simply because I want to make something good even better. An honest appraisal of our institutions is greatly preferable to complacency.

So far I have considered how far the citizen in the Welfare State obtains justice at the hands of tribunals, licensing bodies and local government bodies. I leave to my final lecture the most difficult and important question of all—that is the treatment accorded to the public by the central government machine.

CHAPTER 5

THE CITIZEN AND WHITEHALL

IN this final lecture I shall not of course attempt to cover every aspect of governmental administration. My concern still is with the impact of administrative action on individual citizens. I am not examining the whole process of formulation of governmental policy. I do not regard my subject as a contest between bureaucrat and citizen. All of us, whether members of the public, or Ministers or civil servants, seek the same goal—a manner of arriving at decisions which is fair, and which produces justice for the citizen. I stress once more how vital it is to make the initial procedure as good as possible. That is why in any discussion of the effect of governmental decisions on the citizen one ought first to ask whether the means by which the decision is arrived at must be regulated by law, and, if so, how and to what extent. The second question is to what extent and by whom should that decision be subject to review, that is, how far is some second body to be entitled, at the citizen's request, to take a fresh look at the decision of which he complains. I shall describe the administrative process as it is, and the various ways in which it is supervised, and then consider how far the citizen remains unprotected against possible injustice.

PUBLIC INQUIRIES

The most characteristically British process has been the public inquiry. It is especially important in the two areas which figure so prominently in any discussion of our regulated economy: compulsory acquisition of land and town planning.

Objects of inquiries

Local authorities are entrusted by statute with powers concerning slum property and the provision of housing, but the Department of the Environment's confirmation is ordinarily required before the affected landowner may be deprived of his rights. Other Ministers, such as the Secretary of State for Education and Science with respect to land for schools, are empowered to acquire land compulsorily. Under town planning legislation development plans are prepared which allocate land for residential and industrial use, and which also designate the site of proposed roads, buildings, airfields, parks and open spaces. Anybody who intends to carry out building or other operations on his land, or to change the use to which he puts the land, is subject to planning control. It may be necessary to obtain specific permission before such development is undertaken. The Secretary of State has the final word on such applications, though in the first instance most of them are decided by local authorities.

We accept nowadays that there are circumstances where the needs of the State for land are paramount. We acknowledge that we cannot let every landowner do as he likes with his land regardless of the harm which he might cause to the common weal. At the same time we insist that the State must not arbitrarily deprive the landowner, either of the ownership of his property, or of his freedom to use it as he wishes. A landowner, who objects to compulsory acquisition or whose proposals to develop are resisted by the planning authority, is entitled to demand a public local inquiry. (In many planning cases the Secretary of State now invites the parties to dispense with an inquiry, and instead to have the case decided on the basis of written representations.)

Procedure at inquiries

The public inquiry is conducted in the locality by a civil servant, called an inspector, from the appropriate Department. Parties may be represented by lawyers, evidence may be given and witnesses cross-examined. Ultimately the inspector makes a report to his Department in Whitehall in which he records the evidence, his findings of fact and his recommendations. The Department has private written arrangements which prescribe the status of those civil servants who are to consider the particular report. The file is considered within the Department by the civil servants designated by those arrangements, and ultimately a decision is given in the name of the Minister.

Judicial review

Decisions arrived at in this way have been very frequently challenged in the courts. The landowner's attack has been ostensibly on the procedure. Should the Minister be entitled to discuss with the local authority this matter awaiting decision, or indeed any aspect of the local authority's housing programme, before issuing his decision on a compulsory purchase order? Should the inspector have to disclose his report to the landowner? Should the Minister be prohibited from getting any evidence beyond that in the report? If so, what kind of evidence? New facts or expert advice? Must he give objectors the chance to challenge that further evidence? Should the Minister give reasons? Although these are the principal questions with which the courts have been concerned when called upon to review these compulsory purchase orders the landowner has usually been resisting expropriation simply because the scale of compensation for compulsory acquisition has in his view been less than the market value of his land. And the issue in planning control cases too is normally financial: the landowner who wants to obtain a much higher price for his land by selling it for building purposes is the obvious example.

Recent changes

There used to be many valid objections to the system of local inquiries. The government view that they were in no sense judicial, but merely part of the administrative process, had apparently carried the day in the courts. In a case as far back as 1914 the House of Lords had seemed to have recognised that these processes were essentially administrative.[1] Provided that the inquiry itself was conducted in accordance with the statute, the courts from that date onwards would not intefere. No publication of the inspector's report, no disclosure of reasons by the Minister was required. The Ministry could freely consult either local authorities or other Ministries between receipt of the inspector's report and announcement of the decision. Today the position is different. The inspector's report is published; if the Department receive any new evidence on a matter of fact, including expert opinion on a matter of fact, the Minister has to reopen the inquiry. Even the procedure at the inquiry itself is regulated. When a compulsory purchase order is sought the case for acquisition must be made there; local authority representatives are cross-examined. If other government departments have expressed views an objector can insist on a representative of that department attending the inquiry to give evidence and be cross-examined. The Minister must give a reasoned decision which the courts may review on issues of law.

What has brought about this dramatic improvement? Primarily the Franks Report in 1957. Every one of these

[1] *Local Government Board* v. *Arlidge* [1915] A.C. 120.

changes was proposed in that powerful and convincing Report. It is greatly to the credit of the Government that so many of the Franks proposals were implemented, although it involved an abandonment of the firmly held view of the civil service that these matters should be regarded as in no way judicial, but purely administrative. Further, the Council on Tribunals has been at its best in supervising the handling of inquiries, and its tenacity has led to successive governments implementing the Franks proposals more thoroughly than would otherwise have been the case.

I do not want to weary you with all the detailed case-law about inquiries. The big question is whether this recent tightening in the supervision of the process is desirable. Some say that it is a misguided attempt to impose the procedures of courts on what is a piece of administrative machinery. I do not agree. Administrators are now more careful than before with inquiries. Even so cases have come before the courts recently which show the Department of Housing in an unfavourable light. Take a case in 1967 where the Minister dismissed an appeal by a site owner from a local authority's refusal of planning permission. The Divisional Court of the Queen's Bench Division quashed the Minister's decision because much of his statement of reasons was irrelevant and his letter of decision in general was so obscure that the owner would not know what were the Minister's reasons and what matters he did and did not take into account.[2] The Council on Tribunals has also reported cases of ministerial errors, even when parties have agreed to use the written representations procedure. No doubt many more errors of this kind went undetected before inquiries were brought under super-

---

[2] *Givaudan & Co. Ltd.* v. *Minister of Housing and Local Government* [1967] 1 W.L.R. 250.

vision. If the outcome of a process may be to take away a citizen's land or to diminish its capital value the law must take care that the process is fair. It is legitimate to ensure that the citizen has the chance to know the case against him and then to attempt to rebut it, and that the facts and law on which the decision is based are correct.

Outstanding problems

There are long and inexcusable delays within the Department in disposing of compulsory purchase and planning inquiries, delays so long that they hinder proper implementation of policy. For example, it has been taking almost a year to dispose of every appeal on planning development. The problem is a big one: in a single year there may be 600,000 planning applications and about 20,000 appeals to the Minister. The mistake has been that too few personnel have been engaged to handle these inquiries. And I do not mean merely too few inspectors: the delays in Whitehall after the inspector has reported have been more grievous than those in setting up inquires after objections have been lodged.

I am not starry-eyed about the recent improvements I have mentioned. Whitehall holds the master cards, and no doubt can manipulate the form and content of its decisions so as to make them largely safe from judicial interference in the important matters, even though some of those decisions might be objectionable in their results. Many successful appeals to the courts only touch the trimmings of a Whitehall decision, and do not in the end prevent the Ministry from attaining its substantive aim. Some say that the introduction of safeguards and facilities for judicial review slows up the process unreasonably. It may well be that many inquiries of a type which the Minister conceived as opportunities for citizen's merely to let off steam have nevertheless had the elements of a judicial hearing grafted on to them by the courts. Perhaps many objectors go to the courts just to buy time. Yet the courts will not hesitate, if asked, to stop delaying tactics of that kind by striking out applications as frivolous or vexatious—in 1968 they struck out, for example, Essex County Council's attempted challenge to the Stansted inquiry. When the Department of the Environment has allowed local authorities to stave off for a year or two the inevitable surrender of some of their powers by contesting, even as far as the House of Lords, the schemes designed to transfer their powers to larger authorities, the Department has had only itself to blame for not ending that procrastination by asking the courts to strike out frivolous and vexatious actions.

I would also agree that nothing has been done to improve the quality of the administrative process at its earliest stage. When for instance the local authority resolves to set in motion a clearance scheme in a particular area, the law does nothing to ensure that the choice of area by the local authority is made for the right reasons. For example, a local authority may postpone clearance in Area A and proceed with another scheme in Area B because there are so many coloured residents in Area A that, upon clearance of that slum area, it would have to rehouse them on municipal housing sites, whereas it prefers to contain them within the existing low-grade housing in multiple occupation.

Despite such limitations on the law's efficiency, I insist that the law can play an important part. It must ensure that there is a fair inquiry: the citizen must be given a reasoned decision and a full finding of facts must be published. Compliance with these legal requirements greatly reduces the risk of arbitrary or erroneous decisions. The civil servant's knowledge that part of his handiwork is subject to scrutiny by High Court judges will make him take more care over the quality of his decision.

New reforms

In the last few years successive Governments have made a sustained effort by legislative changes to improve inquiry procedures. Public dissatisfaction with the long delays in handling the greatly increased numbers of applications for permission to develop sites has forced the Government to act. In consequence inspectors may now dispose finally of certain planning appeals without sending in reports and recommendations to Department headquarters. The kinds of case it has in mind are applications to build one house, or those which relate to small sites for residential development or caravans. This belated acceptance of what the Franks Committee recommended is welcome. What is even more significant is the change of heart on the part of the Department which it reveals. The Department has always previously insisted that all planning decisions involve issues of policy which can only be resolved within the anonymity of Whitehall, and that the Minister must assume ultimate responsibility for all planning decisions, however many civil servants participate in the decision process. All of this is tacitly given up when the final decision by a named inspector who has himself conducted the appeal is accepted, as it has been since the 1968 Town and Country Planning Act.

There have also been changes in the law on the handling by local authorities of initial planning applications. Legally, the decision always used to be in the hands of the council of the local authority. What happened in practice was that 60 per cent. to 70 per cent. of all those applications were effectively decided by a paid official whose recommendations were rubber-stamped by his town planning committee. Further trouble has arisen from the frequency with which these officers give informal information or advice with a view to helping members of the public. The official might write to an inquirer that he did not need planning permission for a particular business activity. Relying on this, a citizen might spend a great deal of irrecoverable money in setting up a business. Ultimately, he was ordered by the local authority to stop and dismantle because he had no planning permission. The courts have held that the local planning authority was not bound by letters sent out by its senior officers, and that its freedom to enforce its own planning decisions without compensating the aggrieved citizen was unimpaired by what its officer had previously done or said. Now local authorities can delegate decision-making responsibilities to their chief officers. Of course if they do that it would obviate some of the difficulties I have just been talking about. In practice local government bodies have disappointed the Department by their tardiness in implementing this provision despite a succession of departmental circulars pressing them to delegate much more. Departments are trying hard to reduce delays but local authorities, and perhaps their officials, seem reluctant to heed these governmental recommendations. It is perhaps understandable that local government officials do not welcome this additional task in an area where suspicion of corruption and favouritism is so widespread.

At present there is a lot of dissatisfaction among citizens, who feel that planning decisions which closely affect them are arrived at without their either knowing about them or having adequate opportunity to object. First, it can easily happen that a neighbour makes an application for development without an affected landowner knowing anything about it. A man might want to build a large garage alongside his house close to his neighbour's boundary. He can seek and get planning permission even though neither he nor the planning authority has told the man next door anything about it. It seems odd that if there is an appeal to the Minister followed by an inquiry the citizen who was not entitled to know of the original application is allowed complete freedom to participate in the inquiry. It is even more curious that if he then wants to challenge in the courts what has happened at the inquiry or subsequently in Whitehall he will not be allowed to do so.

You may have heard of the *Chalkpit* case about fifteen years ago—that was one of the grievances in that case. A firm wanted to dig chalk on their land in Essex and appealed to the Minister against the local authority's refusal of permission. One of the objectors at the public inquiry was Major Buxton. He owned an estate of 250 acres nearby and complained that the chalk dust would cause serious damage to his agricultural interests. The inspector agreed and recommended the dismissal of the firm's appeal. The Ministry of Housing consulted the Ministry of Agriculture, Fisheries and Food behind the back of Major Buxton and the other objectors, and then, disregarding the inspector's recommendation, upheld the firm's appeal. Major Buxton challenged in the High Court the legality of the Minister's decision on the ground that the Minister was not entitled after the receipt of the report to obtain other evidence without affording objectors the opportunity to reply to it. The Minister argued that Major Buxton had no standing to challenge his decision—he was a mere outsider—the High

Court agreed with the Minister and dismissed Buxton's suit without going into the merits of his argument.[3]

I said earlier that the procedures at inquiries had been improved recently. These improvements do not apply to all kinds of planning inquiry. Take the case in 1968 when Essex County Council challenged in the High Court the conduct of the Minister of Housing and Local Government over the inquiry into the siting of the third London airport at Stansted.[4] The county council's objection was that before making a special development order for Stansted (under the Town and Country Planning Act 1962), the Minister had taken into account new facts which had not been put in at the inquiry. The council never had the chance to controvert these points of substance. The High Court upheld the Ministry's contention that the council's suit was an abuse of the processes of the court, because in this type of proceeding the Ministry could do as it liked. Another exception is where the Secretary of State for the Environment plans a motorway along a certain route—obviously the business interests of persons whose land will not in itself be acquired may be materially prejudiced. The Secretary of State can please himself whether to hold an inquiry, and if he does, none of the procedural rules I have been talking about binds him in the conduct of that inquiry.

One other important problem which has not been solved satisfactorily is how to deal with questions of alternative sites. It is always relevant at an inquiry to consider whether the case has been made out for compulsory acquisition of land, whether it be for a school, or municipal housing, or highways,

---

[3] *Buxton* v. *Minister of Housing and Local Government* [1961] 1 Q.B. 278.

[4] *Essex County Council* v. *Minister of Housing and Local Government* (1968) 66 L.G.R. 23.

or airports. But how should the Department proceed when an objector accepts the need but disputes the suitability of the proposed site and reinforces it by suggesting an alternative one? The Departments have no procedures geared to meet this problem.

Despite these reservations the public local inquiry is a unique aspect of our administrative process of which we can be proud. It works well, and it has been improved greatly in the last few years. The improvements have been brought about in part by a welcome and perhaps unprecedented collaboration of civil servants and interested legal experts. It is to be hoped that other governmental departments will see the advantages of holding conferences with interested outside bodies at which tough administrative problems can be examined and reforms worked out. The part played by Justice, an association of lawyers, in bringing about these reforms merits special commendation. I am sure that the public local inquiry will continue to serve us well in the future.

Decisions by Civil Servants without a Hearing

Important and extensive though the public inquiry is, a large number of other decisions about claims of individuals is taken by Government without inquiry or any other statutory procedure. The Home Office may refuse to admit an alien or it may deport one. The Foreign Office refuses or withdraws a passport. The Secretary of State for Education and Science will not allow a parent to send a child to the school of his choice, or controls the awards of State studentships to post-graduate university students. The Secretary of State for Social Services decides whether husband or wife is entitled to family allowances. He resolves who shall have mechanically propelled invalid carriages or a grant towards a garage for one, or whether a person is to have a free hearing aid. How much a day in foreign currency is a businessman to be allotted for his trip abroad? How are scarce telephones to be allotted among those on the waiting list? Or beds in public hospitals? I have mentioned before the array of licensing functions vested in Departments, especially the Department of Trade and Industry.

Some needed reforms

Is it satisfactory that in every one of these matters which closely affect the rights of citizens under the Welfare State—and I could greatly add to the list—the citizen should be without the right to be heard, to be given reasons, to appeal, to know who decides, to know what principles, if any, have guided decisions? I cannot believe that the answer to my question is always Yes. Nor can I agree with those whose solution is to set up some new general tribunal to deal with this miscellany.

I repeat what I have said before in these lectures: that each of these instances calls for separate detailed investigation of a kind never carried out up to now, followed by recommendations for change. Obviously some of the matters detailed above should be dealt with by newly constituted special tribunals—the decisions about aliens are the most obvious. In other cases where the Minister in fact works to certain principles they should be published so that an applicant knows what are the relevant criteria: invalid carriages and repayment of contributions to those who mistakenly believed their voluntary national insurance contributions would qualify them for a retirement pension are examples. One of the most significant aspects of the annual reports of the Parliamentary Commissioner (which I shall be talking about later) is the frequency with which he is told that the Minister has internal and unpublished detailed arrangements which were applied to settle so many of these matters. He does not seem in the least disturbed that they decide citizens' claims according to rules which they conceal from citizens: I am. There should always be the right to make some form of representation. I believe that nothing improves the quality of decision-making so much as having to make a finding of facts and a statement of reasons: this principle is applicable to government departments. In many cases the Department has secret arrangements within its hierarchy for handling cases. Certain classes of cases are decided by higher executive officers, others by principals and so on. If a dissatisfied claimant is persistent enough he will have his appeal from the decision heard by a superior in the civil servant hierarchy according to a system clearly laid down within the department. On the other hand the poor uninformed citizen will be told nothing of this opportunity for review of the decision against him arrived at by a civil servant of fairly low grade, and therefore will not have his case reconsidered. As Sir Thomas Beecham said: " The Music of Sibelius is appreciated in Britain because it is like the British Government: reticent and slow of delivery." There seems no excuse for this kind of secrecy. I protest against the complete lack of system in the administrative process as well as against the secrecy. Procedures vary from department to department for no apparent reason other than historical accident. It is nobody's business to oversee the administrative process as a whole, to co-ordinate the work of the various governmental agencies.

A few years ago a committee of lawyers, headed by Sir John Whyatt and set up by Justice, looked at this problem and reported in favour of many of these decisions either being taken away from government departments or at least being subject to an appeal from the department to an outside body. They appeared to subscribe to the view that the kinds of decisions I am discussing should never rest ultimately with a department. I disagree with that generalisation. I am quite prepared to find that certain kinds of hierarchic appeals within departments like Trade and Industry are competently handled. If the changes I have advocated just now are made, I see no reason why a government department should not sometimes be regarded as a suitable body to take ultimate decisions which bear on the rights of individuals.

Control by the courts and its inadequacy

Anyone discussing the efficiency and fairness of the administrative process in relation to the individual must look closely at the part played by the ordinary courts. For the essence of our system is that the courts are the ultimate guardians of our rights and freedoms. They are there to see that Government toes the line, that the Administration dispenses justice to citizens, and they must have the power to intervene effectively where that does not happen. The courts are always empowered to interfere if a department has acted beyond the powers entrusted to it by Parliament. If for instance Parliament sanctioned compulsory purchase orders of houses, but not of parkland, the court would hold invalid a Minister's orders which also embraced parkland.

My comment in an earlier lecture on the clumsiness of the remedies available against tribunals and the need for simplification is equally applicable here. The courts should always be authorised to interfere whenever the Minister is wrong in law. They can do so with regard to housing and town planning orders where, it will be recalled, the Minister must give reasons for either making or refusing the order. Unfortunately, as I have mentioned, government departments are very seldom required to give reasons. Still less is there always an appeal to the courts if the law applied within the department is unsound. This could easily be remedied, and should be. That is one reason why I have pressed that those decisional powers which remain with Ministers should entail the disclosure of their findings of fact and the publication of reasons. That leaves the way open for the courts to do what so often they are at present unable to do, namely, to ensure that whenever a decision by the Government prejudices a citizen, the law has been applied correctly. When a body fails to give a fair hearing upon being required to do so the courts can quash the decision. Thus, planning decisions can be quashed when evidence is taken behind the back of a party. Unfortunately, the courts cannot interfere in this way with governmental decisions unless Parliament has required the Government to observe fair procedures. Too often Parliament has said nothing; this is why it is important that the procedures to be followed for giving the citizen a fair trial should be set out explicitly. If this were done the standards of administration would be raised.

Recently—and the trend is welcome and important—the courts have been insisting that Ministers exercise their discretionary powers in a manner consistent with Parliament's intention. For instance, when the Minister of Agriculture, Fisheries and Food refused to appoint a committee of investigation into a complaint about a milk marketing scheme the House of Lords ordered him to do so because his refusal frustrated the policy of the Agricultural Marketing Act.[5] If a private person, or even a local authority, is acting illegally

[5] *Padfield* v. *Min. of Ag., Fish. and Food* [1968] A.C. 997.

to the detriment of the citizen, the aggrieved citizen can obtain from the courts an injunction to prevent the continuance of the illegal conduct. Unfortunately, in England, but not for instance in Australia, no injunction can be issued against the Crown or a government department.

Again, where one person negligently harms another that other can usually recover compensation in the courts. We can all see that a citizen may suffer through careless behaviour of civil servants. They may lose his application for a licence, so that he cannot start in business. They may negligently give him wrong advice about when and how he should claim some welfare benefit: by the time he learns from another source what his rights are he will be too late to apply. So far the courts have never been willing to hold the Government liable in damages to him for negligence of this kind. No doubt any future claims of this type would be strongly resisted in the courts by the Government. I believe that this is an injustice. It is open to the courts without aid from Parliament to hold that whenever any civil servant or department negligently inflicts financial loss on a member of the public he has a remedy in damages. The courts have not so far even held that if a civil servant maliciously deprives a citizen of a welfare benefit, he has a right to be compensated.

It is a trite observation that the more feeble the performance of the courts in supervising all aspects of the Welfare State the greater is the need for supplementary forms of protection. The pressure for a Parliamentary Commissioner, or Ombudsman, would not have been so insistent if the courts had done all they should. I give one further example—a 1964 case which many regard as one of the most important ones on judicial review of administrative acts decided in the last few years. Mr. Punton worked at Cammell Laird's shipyard at Birkenhead. Two unions were involved in a demarcation dispute. Mr. Punton was a member of neither union and was not even eligible for membership. The union dispute led to a strike. Mr. Punton lost five weeks' work and was refused unemployment benefit. Not surprisingly, he was indignant at being deprived of benefit and appealed to the High Court for a declaration of the law on this vital issue of principle, which had never been decided by the courts previously. The case went to the Court of Appeal which held that it could not even consider his appeal. It refused to hear his claim because it said that even if it declared that he was right in law the Ministry would be unable to pay him—it accepted the Ministry's argument that the Ministry had no authority to pay benefit unless an official award in his favour by a Ministry officer or tribunal had been made.[6] I thought at the time that this decision was singularly unhelpful and legally unnecessary. Candour compels me to say that the judge was a Liverpudlian.

Now look at what has happened with the Parliamentary Commissioner. The same set of tribunals denied a 68-year-old pensioner in Cornwall her full rate of retirement pension. The Parliamentary Commissioner disregarded their rulings and said that she was entitled, and this same Ministry, the Ministry of Social Security, subsequently on the order of the Treasury paid her the £600 in question. What better example could you have of judicial timidity making other supplementary remedies necessary?

Ministerial responsibility—its limitations

Governments are prone to assert that the present remedies of the citizen are adequate, because in the end he enjoys the

---

6 *Punton* v. *Ministry of Pensions and National Insurance* (*No.* 2) [1964] 1 W.L.R. 448.

benefit of the doctrine of ministerial responsibility. Whatever is done by an official, there is, so the argument runs, always a Minister accountable to Parliament.

Ministerial responsibility is reinforced by the great British institution, the parliamentary question. Any M.P. is free to ask a question in the House of Commons of the appropriate Minister about any conduct of any official under the control of that Minister. This system has many merits, but it is not an effective means of remedying large numbers of individual grievances. Question time is short and progress so slow that a Member will be lucky if he can confront a Minister at all. The large majority of questions which call for an oral answer do not get it; there is no time. A Minister can refuse to answer a question, and often does refuse. When he does answer, the civil servant, who has drafted his reply, will have taken every care to give away as little information as possible, and to protect the reputation of his Minister. And even if something has gone wrong within the department, for which the Minister accepts responsibility, almost never does he resign—no doubt because it would be unfair to damage his political career merely because one of his underlings made an error of which he could not be expected to know. With the increasing tendency towards huge departments like those of the Environment and Trade and Industry, it would be absurd to hold the Secretary of State personally accountable for everything in his Department, and everyone knows and accepts it. The further defect is that the M.P. does not know what questions to ask—he has no access to departmental files, and a Minister will not even disclose the contents of files in the course of answering a question in Parliament. There is a simple explanation why the myth of the effectiveness of this device has persisted: it suits Ministers because it appears to be subjecting them to control by Parliament, although the reality is very different; it flatters the ego of back-bench M.P.s who wish to feel that they are more than rubberstamps for their party.

THE PARLIAMENTARY COMMISSIONER

Other countries of the world have felt the need to introduce another safeguard, the Ombudsman. For many years in all the Scandinavian countries this official of Parliament has provided independent supervision of any governmental action which affects citizens. New Zealand introduced this system in 1962. We followed suit with the Parliamentary Commissioner Act 1967.

Scope

The Parliamentary Commisisoner for Administration, at first Sir Edmund Compton, until he was succeeded by Sir Allan Marre in 1971, is in effect appointed by the Government and removable only by Parliament. The nature of his office is essentially the same as that of the Ombudsman elsewhere: the investigation of a citizen's grievances against an official and the expression of a conclusion on that grievance. The case for a Parliamentary Commissioner is the stronger the more gaps there are in the existing protection for the citizen. We have seen that there are many such gaps; to the extent that the Commissioner is able to redress grievances which at present would otherwise go unremedied he must be welcomed.

Unfortunately, our Act is a half-hearted affair, hinged about with restrictions and exceptions. The only person who can complain is the aggrieved citizen himself; unless he is dead or unable to act for himself, nobody can represent him. Local authorities and other public bodies cannot complain. As a sop to M.P.s, a restriction is introduced which other countries have successfully done without. No citizen can complain to the Commissioner direct; he must find an M.P. who is willing to support the request for an investigation. The deterrent effect of this is obvious. It has had another consequence. Of the first 849 cases of complaint completed, 561 were outside the Commissioner's jurisdiction, and even now the Commissioner has to decline to act in 50 per cent. of the cases referred to him because they are outside his jurisdiction. It frequently happens that an M.P. gets publicity for announcing his intention of referring a case to the Commissioner, when it is plain that it will be outside the Commissoner's scope.

Exceptions

The Act has a long list of exceptions which the Commissioner cannot investigate, and he alone decides whether a complaint falls within this list. This list is so long that it covers most of the matters about which citizens complain. Action taken for the purposes of investigating crime or of protecting the security of the State, including action so taken with respect to passports, is excluded. All commercial contracts are excluded, and so questions about defence contracts would be outside his scope. The exercise of the prerogative of mercy, the awards of honours cannot be complained about. Extradition and any matter about foreign affairs are outside his scope. Dr. Soblen's allegation that the Conservative Government extradited him because President Kennedy asked Mr. Macmillan to do so could not be investigated. All questions of appointment or dismissal from the armed forces, the civil service or any public office are excepted. The Commissioner cannot look at any question relating to the administration of justice, and the Lord Chancellor has made it clear that he will not remove that exception. All nationalised industries are excluded. Complaints about the Post Office with respect to the mail and telephones are forbidden. Obviously, to exclude the courts, the police, commercial dealings, and all appointments and dismissals is to impair greatly the usefulness of the Commissioner, as any experienced Citizens' Advice Bureaux worker would confirm. I find many of the exclusions indefensible, especially the police, and the postal and telephonic services.

If the aggrieved citizen has or had a right of appeal to any tribunal or if he has or had a remedy in any court of law, the Commissioner will not investigate. He has a discretion (which he has said that he will exercise only exceptionally) to do so, however, if satisfied that in the particular circumstances it is not reasonable to expect the complainant to resort to the tribunal or the courts. This provision is disturbingly vague; presumably the burden of proof is on the citizen, but how can one decide whether a citizen will win in court if one has to take into account the Government's habitual refusal to produce files in court and the difficulty of knowing whether the court will, at the citizen's request, make the Government produce them. Is " reasonable " subjective? Does one distinguish the wealthy businessman and the poor humble ignorant citizen? Notice that if the citizen had the right to have his case considered by a tribunal, which proceeded to dismiss it, and no right to have that unfavourable decision reversed by the ordinary courts, his complaint cannot be considered by the Commissioner.

The Act also excluded the whole of the hospital service. The National Health Service Reorganisation Act 1973 now creates a Health Service Commissioner (who, initially, is to be the Parliamentary Commissioner) to investigate complaints about National Health Service Hospitals, but the exceptions in the Act are so wide as to make it unimportant. Not only does the exception for courts and tribunals set out in the last paragraph apply, but also no complaints about diagnosis or treatment of patients arising from the exercise of clinical judgment are allowed.

The 1967 Act did not apply to local government, but the Local Government Act 1974 sets up Commissioners for Local Administration along lines similar to the 1967 Act. This belated recognition by Government that the objections to the exclusion of hospitals and local government were valid, is welcome. Perhaps the new proposals by the Home Secretary about police complaints will obviate the need to bring them within the Commissioner's jurisdiction.

Maladministration

I have left to the last the most controversial exception, tucked away in the interpretation section at the end of the Act.

> "It is hereby declared that nothing in this Act authorises or requires the Commissioner to question the merits of a decision taken without maladministration by a government department or other authority in the exercise of a discretion vested in that department or authority."

It is not enough that the citizen has suffered an injustice at the hands of a government department or official; there must also be maladministration, and the Commissioner cannot question the merits of any departmental exercise of discretion taken without maladministration. Even with the most liberal interpretation of maladministration, this would be a serious restriction on the scope of the Act. I will consider shortly how it has been applied.

Other defects in the Act

There are other serious defects in the Act. It prevents the Commissioner from communicating reports of his decisions to the Press. Presumably Parliament did this to preserve its own dignity—the Commissioner has to make a report at least annually to Parliament, which refers it to a Select Committee on the Parliamentary Commissioner. Everybody is precluded from revealing anything the Commissioner says to that Committee—it is a breach of parliamentary privilege for which the House of Commons is empowered to imprison the sinner. The reports of the Commissioner to Parliament contain only summaries of some selected cases, which form a small proportion of the total cases referred to him. Therefore the public has to rely on the accident of whether the objector or his M.P. passes on the Commissioner's decision to the Press. The obstacles to publicity reach the point of absurdity when the Act protects the M.P. from the law of libel in passing on the Commissioner's report to the citizen, but gives no protection to the citizen who then passes it on to the Press. As one would have expected, countries like New Zealand publish detailed accounts of Commissioners' decisions.

An appraisal of the Commissioner's performance so far

Those who have studied other countries' systems have found certain provisions to be of the essence of a successful Ombudsman scheme. The problems are overwhelmingly legal in scope and the Ombudsman has uniformly been a high-ranking jurist totally independent of the civil service, who could also be relied on to make a closely reasoned analysis of his cases and material summaries of the facts. We are paying the price for this lack of a lawyer at the top. In only the second report of the Commissioner—one devoted to noise of jet aircraft at Heathrow airport—the account of the legal position is meagre, totally lacks legal analysis and fails to investigate at all the legal issues which mattered. The same defects are found in dealing with many of the legal problems which dominate the cases summarised in the Commissioner's Reports. No more could be expected of a non-lawyer, but it simply will not do. It is believed that there are other more serious consequences, namely, the Parliamentary Commissioner is being driven to ask Government Ministers like the Attorney-General for advice on how to handle complaints against his Government. Other staffing errors have been made. We are told that the rest of the staff consists almost entirely of junior civil servants, members of the executive class, and—incredible as it may seem—that there is not a single lawyer on his staff. How can they be expected fearlessly and ruthlessly to probe into the activities of other departments when, after secondment for a year or so to the Commissioner's office, they expect to seek promotion within perhaps the very departments with whose maladministration they are now concerned?

Experts also agree that the Ombudsman should have power to proceed on his own initiative without waiting for a complaint—that is how much of the best work is done. The Parliamentary Commissioner is forbidden to do that.

Most of the criticisms I have so far advanced have not been against the way in which the Commissioner is operating the Act. Regrettably criticism must go further. We all know that one of the chronic weaknesses of the civil service is its slowness; this also shows up time and time again in the Commissioner's Reports. One thing above all is required of the Commissioner—that he should act swiftly. Yet the Commissioner has brought to his office the habits acquired from his life as a civil servant. Right from the start all sign of urgency has been missing—it is significant that his reports are silent on the size of his delays in handling cases. If a complaint is outside his jurisdiction I would say that that ruling ought to be communicated within seven days of receipt of the claim—yet incredibly M.P.s complain that months go by without even having their reference acknowledged. The Commissioner's procrastination is all the more serious when another of the Act's provisions is noted; the department is free to carry on with any further action it thinks fit, even though the Commissioner is conducting his investigation and even if it has reason to believe that the Commissioner is about to find maladministration.

Other civil service attitudes are discernible in the first reports. The Act appoints the Commissioner for the benefit of the citizen and of nobody else. He should establish a rapport with the public. It is therefore unfortunate that his reports are not written in a way which would make it attractive for the general reader. They smack of governmental reports when they should have had the flavour of say Alastair Cooke. All the familiar civil service language is there: "I have not thought it appropriate for me to," "It will be for consideration whether," "I need not add that." This civil service mind is seen in other aspects of the reports. In the very first paragraph of his first Annual Report on the results of his work he went out of his way to say that none of the maladministration was of "a seriously culpable character." The emphasis is on whitewashing the civil service. But what concern are those issues of blameworthiness to the man with a grievance? If there is incompetence or inefficiency, and he has lost something because of it, that is what he is complaining about. The focus should surely be on whether maladministration has caused injustice to the individual, not on whether the reputation of the civil servant remains untarnished. I am not saying that the Parliamentary Commissioner should not seek to improve the performance of the civil service; of course he should suggest ways in which civil service procedure can be changed for the benefit of the citizen and the country. He will succeed in these respects only if he defines maladministration widely; if he requires the civil service to decide cases within weeks, not years, if he requires them, upon a citizen's request, to give full reasons in writing, if he insists on their stating the principles and procedures according to which they are working in particular areas, and identifying those who make the decisions. This he is failing to do.

His Reports abound with examples of failure by civil servants to disclose the regulations according to which decisions are being made—for example, on late claims for cereal subsidies, on making improvement grants for farm equipment, on grants for post-graduate study, on investment grants by the Board of Trade, on the acquisition of gold coins. Yet there is no attempt to encourage the publication of these secret arrangements which determine the citizen's rights.

The Commissioner is supervised by a Select Committee of the House of Commons on the Parliamentary Commissioner for Administration. The Committee soon criticised his narrow interpretation of " maladministration "; he was satisfied with decisions if the procedures were right, and would not consider whether they were manifestly unreasonable or based on mistaken facts. He has been driven by the Committee into taking a slightly wider view; the Committee wish him to infer maladministration from the thoroughly bad quality of a decision and from the failure of a Department to review the working of a rule framed by a Department which is shown repeatedly to cause hardship to individuals. Any assessment of the Commissioner must rest on scrutiny of his published reports. Some were prompted by his willingness to tackle George Brown over the Foreign Office handling of the Sachsenhausen concentration camp case to accord him a most favourable verdict. I thought then and still think that the case was not one on which to base a judgment overall. The reports show that he continues to interpret maladministration narrowly, and when he finds it, as often as not all that emerges, to his but not to public satisfaction, is an expression of official regret or a declaration by a Department that it will review its procedures. All his reports are shrouded in total anonymity; contrast his vague inquiries into the Department of Trade and Industry's handling of insolvent motor insurance companies with the forthright criticism by the special tribunal of inquiry set up to inquire into the handling by the Department of Trade and Industry of the Vehicle and General Insurance Company. Particularly significant is the great decline in the number of cases validly referred to the Commissioner. His supporters will say that this is because he has virtually eradicated the shortcomings of the Administration, the less charitable view is that the public has no confidence in his ability to redress their grievances and that the system is operated so as to make it as likely as possible that they will not trouble him.

If the Commissioner is to be effective he must be a figure in the public eye, he must produce reports which promptly and prominently identify maladministrators, he must produce blueprints for action to remedy proven defects, he must see himself as a defender of citizen's rights not a whitewasher of the civil service, and he must be concerned to deal with delays, negligence and concealment of regulations from the citizen. He must not continue to ignore manifestly unreasonable administrative action. The citizen must have the right to complain to him direct, and on the matters which concern him without that present formidable list of exceptions which meet governmental convenience. The thoroughness which has characterised the Commissioner's investigations shows that the Parliamentary Commissioner system is capable of being transformed into a useful agency for protecting an Englishman's rights.

THE ADMINISTRATIVE PROCESS

Inadequate protection for citizens

Many are dissatisfied with the administrative process itself. They believe that nothing so far discussed acknowledges that the civil service may still make decisions that are unfair or impose a disproportionately great burden on a few citizens. They maintain that the merits of administrative decisions and the methods of the administration should be reviewed by others. They point to the lot of the householder when an overhead motorway is to be built nearby. They ask about those whose land falls under the long shadow of a decision to allocate certain land to industrial use. A Borstal has to be built somewhere; what about those who live in the chosen village? They concede that these decisions may be lawful and arrived at without maladministration, and yet they worry that administrators have the final responsibility for decisions like this which inevitably strike hard and perhaps arbitrarily on the unlucky few.

The argument for a Conseil d'Etat

Two different solutions are canvassed. Some look enviously across the Channel at France's *Conseil d'Etat.* This is a body composed of high-ranking administrators and jurists which has worked out legal principles specially applicable to citizen/State conflicts. Its philosophy is that public law is different from private law and can be developed only by those close to and sympathetic with the administrative process. No doubt the *Conseil d'Etat* is successful (though less so than Frenchmen would have us believe). Yet you cannot easily graft an alien institution onto the existing body. The principles of the *Conseil d'Etat* are so different from the basic ideas of English law that I believe that it would be unwise to introduce them here. There are so many merits in what we have that we should not lightly cast aside our present system. Instead we must be content to amend and improve it.

The argument in favour of an administrative division of the High Court

Others see an analogy in the Restrictive Practices Court formed within the framework of our present system of courts, but composed of both High Court judges and economists, to handle problems of restrictive practice agreements. They would set up a special administrative division of the High Court for problems affecting the State in its relations with citizens. Whenever a body had reached a decision without a hearing this new court would be entitled to make an independent finding of fact. This would fill a gap in the present arrangements, but the gap to be filled would be small if my proposals for increasing the hearing obligations of decision-makers were implemented. I think it more important to have the first decision right than to allow a full rehearing on appeal. They also propose that this court should hear appeals from bodies which have given a hearing or held an inquiry; the need for this would be reduced if the existing forms of judicial review were to be strengthened in the ways I recommend.

The role of Parliament

I admit that there is a problem which England has not solved, but I retain the old-fashioned idea that it is for Parliament to make the fundamental decisions of policy. I am well aware that it is impossible to draw a clear line between those decisions and others which are suitable for adjudication by some judicial process. I recognise that a decision is justiciable even though it may involve some element of policy making and the exercise of discretion. I insist that Parliament should settle basic policies and formulate as sharply as possible the criteria for other bodies to apply in deciding individual cases. Parliament too often shirks this task, and this leads to complaints about the unfairness of the administrative process—complaints which need never have arisen. I do not agree that a reviewing body is always a better decision maker than a government department.

I draw attention to one specific change in the parliamentary process which is urgently needed. In recent years the most unsatisfactory kinds of administrative decision within Ministries have been on such matters as allocation of investment grants—the Parliamentary Commissioner has had complaints in this area but it is not his fault that the arrangements for allocating these grants are so faulty and so resented by industry. The defects result from the fact that these schemes come within the constitutional folklore of the Budget. We are all familiar with the charade annually performed by the

Chancellor of the Exchequer. Nobody is to have the slightest idea of the Budget proposals until he speaks in the House of Commons on Budget day. When therefore he introduces some lengthy complex regulatory scheme like investment grants, all the details have been finalised by him without the possibility of change, without consultation with those who would know better than the Treasury how to do it—industrialists, administrative lawyers, and the Council on Tribunals. It is part of the Budget and therefore secret in every detail. The result is, inevitably, inefficient machinery and widespread injustice. The essential secrecy of the Budget could be retained without continuing to jeopardise the justice of administrative arrangements like these. Schemes of this kind are not formulated overnight; many are considered without being implemented. Their details should never be enacted without the help of those best fitted to advise on their content.

Too often a complaint about an administrative decision is really a criticism of Parliament, justified or otherwise. Take the case of the families who were required by Kent County Council to vacate accommodation in their hostel even though they had no alternative accommodation. Parliament had not imposed a duty on local authorities to house displaced homeless families, nor had it laid down any obligations towards families who were admitted to hostels. If the council in its discretion required occupants to leave after three months the court could not interfere because Parliament left it to the council's discretion.[7] But how could a special administrative court review the decision? It was not contended that the decision was arbitrary. If Parliament did not lay down rules, but chose to entrust the broad discretion to local authorities, what role had a reviewing body if that discretion had been

---

[7] *Kent County Council* v. *Daniels*, *The Times*, May 4, 1966.

fairly applied in the individual case? Contrast that with the *Enfield* case where the plans of Enfield London Borough Council to proceed with comprehensive education were impeded when a few ratepayers sued the council. Once the ratepayers had proved that the council had failed to observe the procedures which Parliament had laid down, the result was inevitable, and surely right.[8] We cannot let local authorities disregard the restrictions which Parliament has attached to the powers conferred on them. It may well be that the *Enfield* case shows that it is difficult to reflect equal concern for the corporate view, and for those who were deprived of schooling temporarily by the court's decision. That may be a fair criticism of the educational administrative process, but I cannot see how we can ever countenance delegates of power from Parliament ignoring the conditions which Parliament had attached to the exercise of that power.

I believe in a multiplicity of safeguards for the citizen. For me it is no criticism of the British system that there is no one way of guarding the citizen's rights—I don't want to entrust the entire responsibility to some some special administrative court. Parliament has a part to play. It must devise procedures which ensure that the fundamental decisions of policy are fairly arrived at. There is room for improvement. The main criticism of matters like Stansted is that inner circles of administrators have advanced too far towards one solution before the inquiry process, which is the first time that the citizens can air their views, is allowed to begin. The Lord Chancellor should have greatly increased powers to bring about more uniformity into the administrative process—he should inculcate standards of fairness and openness which are not now always attained. Our tribunals should be under closer

---

[8] *Bradbury* v. *Enfield London Borough Council* [1967] 1 W.L.R. 1311.

and more continuous scrutiny. We should decide which administrative decisions need to be brought within the tribunal fold. The aim is to ensure that every decision is made by one appropriate and identified body working to fair and open procedures.

The reform of judicial review

I regard the courts as a bulwark of our liberties. Their reviewing powers should be strengthened and simplified. They should be much more willing than they are to compensate the victims of official negligence, delay and incompetence. They can do that without Parliament's help, especially now that it is clear that the courts can insist on the Government's producing documents in its possession even though the Crown refuses on the ground of public interest—it is for the courts to decide whether public interest demands that documents be kept secret. I see merit in the Parliamentary Commissioner, if only his powers were fashioned on the Scandinavian and New Zealand models. He could unearth and expose injustice where the aggrieved citizen was powerless to protect himself. If all these reforms were made, I would be content. I believe that there would be no need to import the *Conseil d'Etat* and no need to interfere further with the administrative decision itself.

We start with the supreme advantage that English administration is exceptionally free from corruption (Poulson notwithstanding). In Parliament, the courts, tribunals, the civil service and the Parliamentary Commissioner, we have the institutions capable of giving the citizen a square deal. Our foundations are sound. The task of ensuring that Englishmen are given justice under the Welfare State is not impossibly difficult. We are justly proud of the concern for individual rights which is so characteristic of our way of life. We must not be complacent. There are improvements to be made, not by throwing away what we have, but by adapting our present institutions. I have tried to point out in detail what changes are necessary. When these are made, we can ensure that our citizens enjoy justice in the Welfare State.